BiLLBOARdS

Written by **Clifford Meth**

Illustrations by **Dave Gutierrez**

KURT VONNEGUT once chided me
for holding back in my stories.
This collection, unrestrained, is for him.

–CM

ISBN: 978-1-60010-422-0

12 11 10 09   1 2 3 4

www.idwpublishing.com

Operations: Ted Adams, Chief Executive Officer • Greg Goldstein, Chief Operating Officer • Matthew Ruzicka, CPA, Chief Financial Officer • Alan Payne, VP of Sales • Lorelei Bunjes, Dir. of Digital Services • AnnaMaria White, Marketing & PR Manager • Marci Hubbard, Executive Associate • Alonzo Simon, Shipping Manager • **Editorial**: Chris Ryall, Publisher/Editor-in-Chief • Scott Dunbier, Editor, Special Projects • Andy Schmidt, Senior Editor • Justin Eisinger, Editor • Kris Oprisko, Editor/Foreign Lic. • Denton J. Tipton, Editor • Tom Waltz, Editor • Mariah Huehner, Associate Editor • **Design**: Robbie Robbins, EVP/Sr. Graphic Artist • Ben Templesmith, Artist/Designer • Neil Uyetake, Art Director • Chris Mowry, Graphic Artist • Amauri Osorio, Graphic Artist • Gilberto Lazcano, Production Assistant

Introduction

The *reductio ad absurdum* — the over-the-top presentation of a satirical idea that goes well beyond normal probability to drive its wicked point home — is an ancient satirical technique. Aristophanes used it 2500 years ago in his anti-war play LYSISTRATA, which told how women could put an end to war by withholding sex from their men. Jonathan Swift, in his essay "A Modest Proposal," suggested that the impoverished Irish could ease their burdens by selling their children to the rich for food. Philip K. Dick's short story "The Pre-Persons," intended to advocate a pro-life stance, proposed that abortion be made legal up to the age when a child learned how to do algebra. Kurt Vonnegut, in Harrison Bergeron, showed us what the world would be like if everybody was made ***really*** equal — in intelligence, in attractiveness, in physical strength, and everything else.

And here comes Clifford Meth now with his own contribution to the literature of over-the-top satire. Vonnegut and Swift would have loved this wicked little story. Marshall McLuhan, too. Philip K. Dick would have sighed and said, "Well, sure. What did I tell you?"

Meth's is a vision of the future that's not really very futuristic, sad to say. The world it predicts may be nearer to becoming real than we'd like to think.

Science fiction is supposed to give us a view of things to come, and, since the cultural matrix that's depicted here does not actually exist yet, I suppose you have to call this a science-fiction story. But only by a whisker or two. The scene it shows is uncomfortably close to present-day reality...and getting uncomfortably closer every hour.

Robert Silverberg

Table of Contents

Foreword

A new collection of stories is always an occasion for a few introductory words from the author, so here are mine:

Everything you are about to read is true. Forget that drivel in the front matter about names, characters, places, institutions, and incidents being products of the author's imagination. That, my friends, is the *only* fiction you'll find between the covers. An author, at least this one, takes the world in through the glass darkly of his own bruised experiences, chews a bit, swallows, then gives you a cud-like product meant to entertain and sometimes enlighten. But it's rarely fiction. It is, rather, regurgitated reality.

Take "Billboards," the opening entrée (to carry the metaphor to its culinary conclusion). This is a story I wrote and first published in 1996, years before Google and Wiki and iPods existed, to say nothing of people selling space on their bodies to corporations. Did I see it coming? Oh, hell—I didn't even see the Great Depression Part II coming until we were burning our comic books just to stay warm. I didn't see the scandalous incompetence of captains of industry until everyone I knew was broke or breaking, but I tapped out "Wagging the CEO" and "Blowing Smoke" a year before Lehman Brothers' collapse marked the opening salvo of Wallstreet's downfall. Like a good amp, I was feeding back; taking in the signals and channeling it to you fine citizens. But it wasn't fiction.

I regard it as something warmer than whimsy, something I'd caught a whiff of and needed to bottle before it tainted everything. The fact that much of what I wrote came true one or two or ten years later just goes to prove my grandfather's old adage even in this new ad age. And that is this: You don't have to stick your nose in dog shit to know that it smells.

Clifford Meth
The Ruins of New Jersey
January, 2009

Billboards

Americans are the media;
And America is the message.
—*John Wayne Nakamura*

Frank Bittle scratched the itchy Exxon Tiger just below his left nipple, then the WalMart logo on the back of his head, and then he sat up. It was a sticky day—a hot, mid-summer bastard though dry, with the sun directly overhead and not a Goodyear cloud in the sky. Frank decided, Bain de Soleil or not, it was time to get out of the sun before he began fading, so he folded his beach towel, IBM spread over Burger King banner, then tossed the towel over his right shoulder, borderline violating his contract with Jack LaLanne, but what the hell, no one was looking.

The white sand was hot beneath his feet as Frank moved along the Margate beach. It was the only shore point in New Jersey left open to the public, the others having gone to sludge and just as well—the State Parks & Rec Department made a fortune leasing the beaches to Bendix and Hoffmann-LaRoche and Beckton-Dickinson for toxic dumping—far more than they'd have pulled in on concession stand rentals and highway tolls and speeding tickets and bribes.

Frank was almost at the boardwalk when he spotted her. His eyes instantly fixed on her faultless, heart-shaped fundament, fully exposed, a turquoise shoelace thong notwithstanding. It was a beautiful sight, a delightful thing to watch, and so he did, Cap'n Crunch on the left cheek, Joe Camel on the right, each bouncing up and down in perfect syncopation. He'd seen more ass than a toilet seat but never anything better. She was about twenty yards from Frank when he decided to turn and follow her. It was a weakness and he knew it. Just couldn't resist a nice ad.

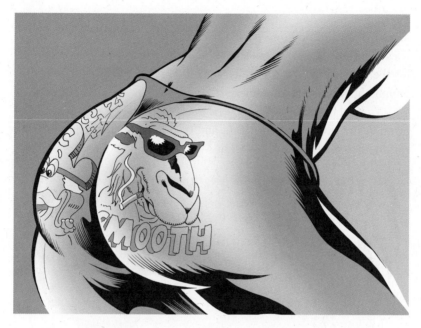

She stopped at the Nathan's Famous stand and ordered a foot-long and a Diet Coke. Then she fixed her lipstick as she waited out the cooling of her foot-long, which was only six-and-five eighth's inches long and, sans relish, about four inches in diameter. By way of comparison, it was roughly the size of her favorite vibrator, a similarity that didn't escape her. Thinking just that, she lifted the dog and blew slightly, then tested its temperature against her Estee Lauder lips.

Frank watched all this as he sauntered up sideways, spider-like, or at least Frank-like. He plucked a stool from the end of the counter and placed it just inches from hers, squatted, and ordered a dog for himself. From the corner of his eye, he watched her crunch an ice cube. Then, when his repast arrived with alacrity, he took a deep breath and turned to her and proclaimed, "I'll show you mine if you show me yours."

With some hesitation, she looked at Frank, then studied him up and down as if he were a dress whose purchase she was considering. Her eyes took in Frank's beefy, muscled body, which flexed slightly beneath a perfect tan and a throng of corporate tattoos. She lingered a moment, blinked several times a pair of long Maybellines over baby blues. "Okay," she said.

Frank grinned his inner triumph. He moved his hand casually across the counter, allowing her to watch his fingers crawl toward her. Then he picked up his hotdog and peeled back the bun, exposing the steaming wiener and the scrawling on its side, a bright yellow-and-green house ad for the Coney Island-born establishment. He rotated the frank with his thumb; the flip side read Meineke Mufflers.

The girl batted her lashes several times, a practiced habit, then looked down at her own dog, exposed it, and held it up for his scrutiny. Frank smiled, then read aloud: "Less filling."

She smiled back. "Tastes great."

"Talk about subliminal," he said. "Now I'm dying for a beer."

"That's not subliminal," she said. "That's overt. You want subliminal?" She bowed her lashes again, keeping the lids shut. On her right eyelid, in Friz Quadrata five-point bold, *Aren't You Hungry?* On the left, *For McDonalds?*

"Cute," he said.

"Six-thousand credits plus frequency bonuses," she said.

"I'm Frank," said Frank, extending his hand, which she took with an athlete's grip. "Angela," she said. She attempted to retrieve her hand from his, but he held fast.

"You're in good hands," he said.

"Oh," she said, getting it, but he exposed his palm anyway and displayed the fluorescent-green message.

"Allstate," he said. "Eight thousand credits plus frequencies. Just made enough on that shake to cover lunch."

"Then cover it," she said, "and let's blow this hot-dog stand."

★ ★ ★

It was cooler as the sun settled down. Frank lay back on the lawn with his hands behind his head, wholly relaxed except when Angela tickled Mr. Clean's head above his pelvic bone. She snuggled beside him, drawing tiny circles with her finger on his abdomen.

"Whatcha' thinking?" It was the first words she'd spoken in the last two hours. They'd made it three times, but her only sounds were guttural pleasure-pain yelps, for which Frank was eternally grateful. If there was one thing he hated in bed, it was a slogan-shouting bitch.

"Frank?"

"Hmm?"

"I said, whatcha' thinking?"

He was thinking that she'd responded like a thoroughbred, though there was something virginal about her, too. "I'm thinking about that sunset," he said, concluding that what he was feeling was a pang of romance and not the Chablis. "I'm thinking that's the nicest sunset I've ever seen."

Angela peered out at the horizon. The sun was a golden orange; it shimmered where it met the landscape creating a startling aurora borealis effect to its the left, and to its right: *This enhanced sunset brought to you by Cadence, makers of superior graphics cards.*

"It's pretty," said Angela. "They do a nice job. I'll always remember them now."

"Hmm?"

"Every time I see a Cadence product," she said, tickling Mr. Clean, "I'll think of you."

Frank smiled. He liked this girl. Most Pro-Duct Femmes were horribly stuck on themselves, silly and selfish, but Angela seemed different. Giving. She'd certainly been giving in bed. Yes, he decided he liked this girl. "Mind if I smoke?" he asked.

"Uhm-mm."

"All I have is store-bought." He got up to roll a joint. "Haven't seen the good stuff in a while."

"Yeah," said Angela. "My dad said grass was better before the government started selling it."

Frank shook his head. "Old people." He sprinkled the tiny green-brown bits onto a leaf of Zig-Zag. "Always saying crap like that. *My* old man?" He ran the glue-side of the rolling paper across his tongue to seal his creation. "Always hankering for the past. The *old* days. Everything was better in the *old* days." Frank withdrew a small lighter from his shorts and lit the joint, inhaling deeply. A sweet, pungent aroma filled the general vicinity. He passed the joint to Angela who took a hit then passed it back.

"Where's your dad now?" She sat up on the air mattress they'd spread across the grass at the rest stop where they'd parked. Her naked body glistened with sweat.

Frank didn't answer. He lay back again and took several deep hits, trying to rush the buzz, until a coughing fit finally put him in the land, well in orbit, with his head all fuzzy and warm. "My old man was really something," he said when the fuzz finally cleared. "An electrical engineer."

"Electrical? Really?" asked Angela, impressed, or just impressed that Frank was impressed.

"Expected me to be one, too," said Frank. He closed his eyes. "Wasn't having any part of it, though. I studied modeling. Knew which side *my* bread was buttered on. I wasn't producing jack."

"Electrical," Angela repeated absently, stoned.

"One of the last, I suppose. Ran out of work before he ran out of steam. With no American companies left to work for, the old man got crispy. Said he'd rather rot than make rice burners."

"Rice burners?" Angela began rubbing oil on her breasts, very sensuously, but Frank didn't notice. He was in the land.

"That's what my old man called anything made outside of America."

"But everything *is* made in America."

"Well, yes and no." He took one last toke, then flicked the roach away. "The old man said there was once a whole bunch of companies, but after a mess of mergers, there were just three left—one in China, one in Korea, and one in Japan. They all agreed to keep long-established American brand names intact. American names are cool. But everything today is made by techno-kamikazes."

Angela looked up at Frank. As their eyes met, she started to laugh. It was a compelling, ticklish giggle that made Frank want her again. "I didn't understand a word you just said."

Frank laughed, too, mostly because he was stoned and he didn't know if he believed any of it either. "Who gives a shit?" he said.

They were both hysterical when a cop approached them. The cop had a nasty look on his face. He held out his open hand to Frank. "This yours?"

Frank looked at the marijuana dog-end. "Yes, sir, officer."

The cop pointed to a sign at the rest stop, not twenty feet away. The sign said *No Littering* and the cop said it, too. "No littering. That's a twenty-five credit fine. Wrist."

Frank obeyed as the policeman reached in his breast pocket and withdrew a small transceiver, which he ran over the barcode tattoo on Frank's wrist. Then the cop turned to Angela. "You should get some clothes on, Miss," he said. "They say it might rain."

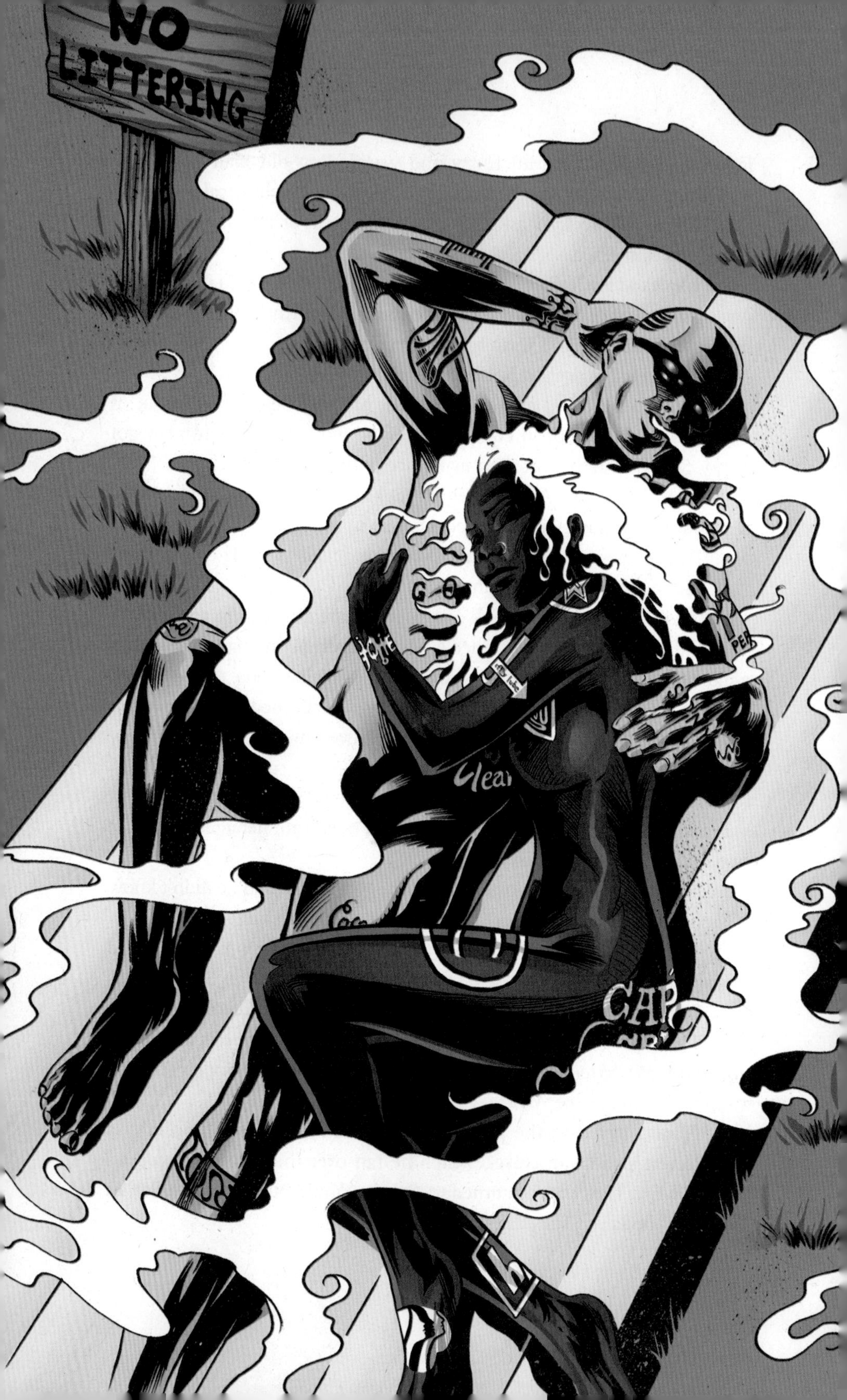
NO LITTERING

They both watched the cop walk away. When he was out of earshot, Frank said, "They're never around when you need them."

★ ★ ★

Frank and Angela were strolling down the boardwalk, hand-in-hand, stoned, when they came across the demonstration.

"Let's cruise," said Frank. He pulled Angela in reverse, but she resisted. "I want to see," she said.

"It's just the Spotless," he said. "Let's get out of here." Frank felt himself tense up and tried to push the apprehension away. *The Spotless.* Demonstrators. Right to Dermisers. Immaculate Peels, as a popular talk-radio host called them. Frank despised the lot of them. He hated anyone undermining the easy life Americans had earned by virtue of birthright or good looks or the ability to hit a round ball with a round bat squarely. By selling space on his skin, Frank had purchased a life of relative ease and relaxation, days of tanning salons and aerobics, evenings of parties and preening and posing for the tourists. Tourists were what Americans called Asians. Frank liked tourists. He thought they were cute little fellas.

"Look at those cute little fellas," he said to Angela as the two walked away from the demonstration and passed a group of camera-popping businessmen. "They don't go anywhere without their cameras."

Angela smiled as Frank flexed his bicep, which coincidentally sported a Nikon ad, for the cute little guys with the cameras. Frank flexed in vain. It was Angela's picture they were taking. Somewhere, data of the incident was received, processed, and logged in multiple redundancy databases.

"I like tourists," said Frank, his muscular arm draped around Angela's waist, his beefy hand brushing Cap'n Crunch. "They're artistic people." Angela snuggled closer and Frank returned the gesture with a playful squeeze on the Cap'n. "Cameras," Frank waxed, "are to Orientals what red noses are to clowns."

At the other end of the boardwalk, another rally was being staged. Frank turned to retreat again, but this time Angela stood her ground. "I'm sick of this!" she said. "What the hell do they have against advertising?"

"That's not it, Angie. There's a lot more to it." He watched the demonstrators—people naked of tats carrying signs that read *America for*

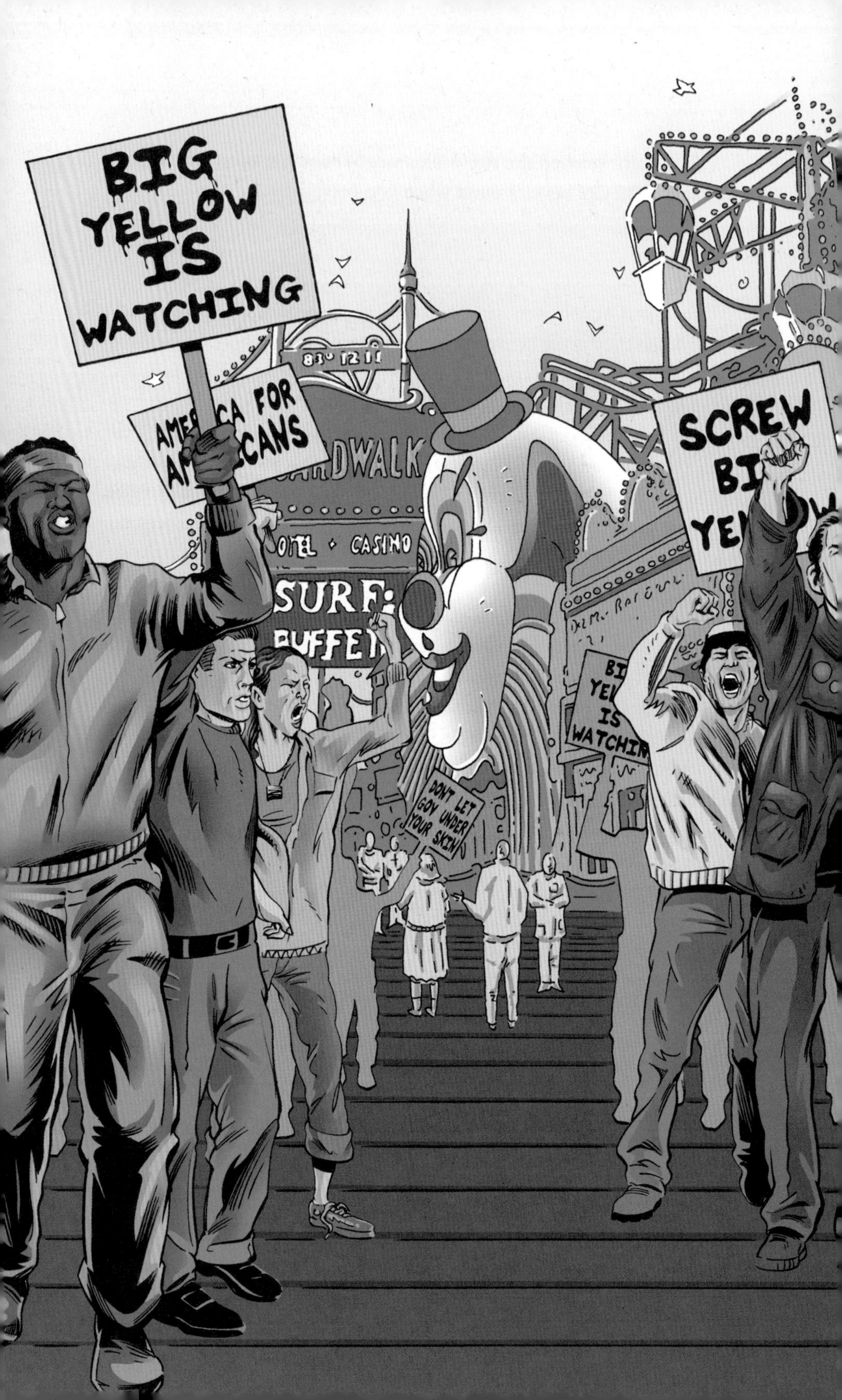
BIG YELLOW IS WATCHING
SCREW
CASINO
SURF:
DON'T LET GOV UNDER YOUR SKIN

Americans, Big Yellow Is Watching, and *Don't Let Government Under Your Skin.*

Frank understood more than he cared to articulate. His father had educated him. He knew it wasn't corp tats being protested—it was the information system built into the skin media, a system that allowed companies to detect whether service levels of agreements were being adhered to. An entire microelectronics network—consisting of intelligent sensors from Motorola, communications protocols from AT&T, and organic semiconductors from Phillips—was micro engineered into every image. The net used skin ducts as its wiring matrix. Each skin-pic, with its own microcontroller and neural transceiver, was integrated with the nervous system. Consequently, when a body did what a body was supposed to do—such as repeat a slogan, or pose for a camera, or eat a brand product—a signal was processed and recorded and tabulated and auto-analyzed for instant reporting. Then the individual was credited by the appropriate company. All in all, it was a perfectly sensible system, thought Frank. Sensible and reliable.

Before Frank could stop her, Angela slipped her hand from his and headed straight toward the demonstrators. She approached a skinny guy with a *Screw Big Yellow* sign. The man was one of a dozen demonstrators marching loudly behind a police barricade. Angela yelled something at the man that Frank couldn't quite make out over the chanting, but the skinny man heard her just fine, stopped marching, and began to shout back.

"You stupid tart!" he screamed. "You're packaged like a fucking candy bar!"

"Keep your laws off my body, fascist!" Angela returned.

"You're a disgrace!" a second protester added, a hard-looking woman with a severe haircut and no makeup. "Corporate tool! Mindless billboard!"

"Go to hell!" Angela yelled, "You can all go straight to hell!"

Frank took her by the hand and dragged her away.

★ ★ ★

It was 2:15 a.m. Frank couldn't sleep. He thought about taking an Extra Strength Halcyon but decided to plug into the virtual instead. He got out of bed and went to the entertainment room, but after twenty minutes found it impossible to concentrate, so he headed back to the bedroom.

"What's wrong?" asked Angela, her pillowed head turned from the door. "Sorry, Angie. Did I wake you?"

"No. Sort of." She sat up. "What's wrong?"

"Can't sleep."

"Want to make love?"

He thought about it, then sighed. "Not really."

"What's bothering you?"

Frank put his hands behind his head and stared at the Trojan ad on the ceiling. "I keep thinking about that demonstration."

At which point Angela came fully awake. "Oh, piss on those losers."

"My old man was one of those losers," said Frank.

"What?" Angela grabbed his hand. "He was there today?"

"No, no." Frank closed his eyes and rubbed them with his fingers. "But he *would've* been. He's been gone a long time now. They sent him to Rahway."

"Wo!" said Angela. "He killed someone, huh?"

Frank smirked. "Murder's still a misdemeanor in Jersey. The old man committed a felony." He scratched the Exxon Tiger beneath his nipple. "Snuck a computer virus into Nippon Steel's system. Cost 'em billions."

"No shit!" said Angela.

"Two back-to-back life sentences. Nothing but no-frills food and public-access television."

"Christ!" said Angela.

The two lay in silence for some time. Then Frank said, "To be honest, I was surprised they caught him. He was one smart sonuvabitch, my old man. Burned out his own barcode and everything. They nicked him while he was giving a lecture at Rutgers." Frank opened his eyes and sat up. "Wanna see it?"

"See what?"

"The lecture," said Frank. "I have it on inst-ROM."

"Is it against the law?"

"Nah. It's public domain data-net. Evidence against a subversive." Frank got out of bed and walked into the entertainment room. Angela followed closely behind. She watched Frank pick up the remote and press a button, then watched as a screen lowered from a panel in the ceiling.

Frank hit another button to access the ROM library, then clicked on the menu and his father emerged in life-size high-def. A closed-caption beneath the image read Dr. William Bittle, chief scientist, Lawrence Livermore Laboratories. Frank hit fast-forward. "I'll skip the boring parts," he said. He accessed the search function and said, "Intel." The racing image in front of him paused. "This is it," he said.

"...Intel first developed the enabling technology that would run polymer-based ICs through the complex network of skin ducts," said Dr. Bittle. "Thus, the term Pro-Ducts. The nickname caught on because yuppies had long considered themselves the only productive members of society and were delighted to tie themselves in with the global powers. Izod shirts gave way to Izod tattoos. Embedded Tagheuer watches were given free to those who allowed the company's logo to be designed onto their wrists...

"The entire marketing ploy," Bittle continued, "was the brainchild of John Wayne Nakamura, son of industrialist trillionaire Hiro Nakamura, C.E.O. of Paramount-Lorimar-Disney-MGM America Ltd. His son, John Wayne, the best-selling author of *Chewing Slowly*, believed that Americans were good for nothing more than conspicuous consumption. We no longer produced anything—we had simply become entertainment and information vendors for the rest of the world. Americans, said John Wayne, are the media. America, said John Wayne, is the message...

"Nakamura was a driven supporter of Pro-Duct technology. He envisioned the skin-duct network as an information superhighway that would be continuously monitored. Today, huge terabit databases do just that in Tokyo, Seoul, and Beijing. Asian product managers receive perpetual reportage on every byte of marketable

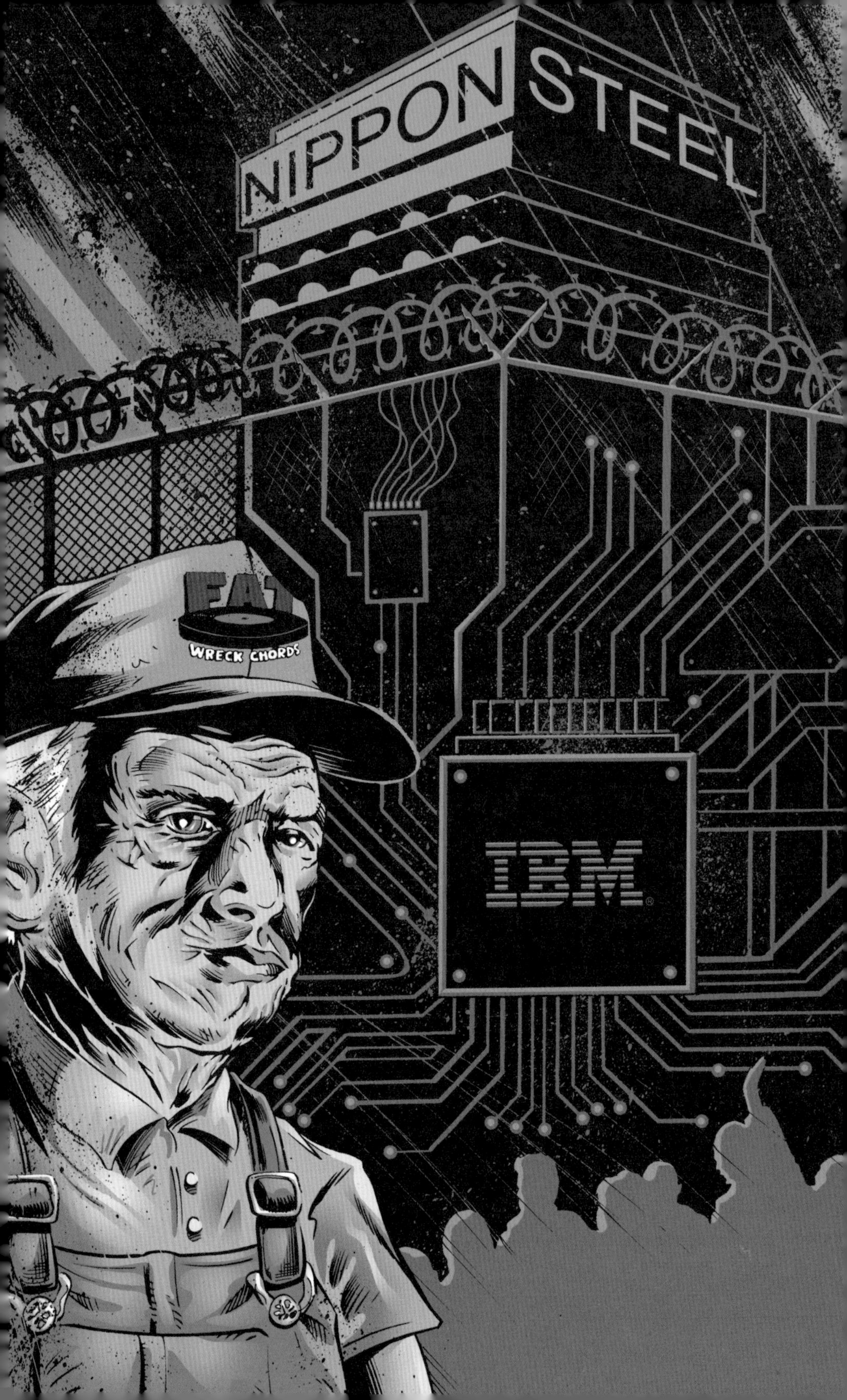
NIPPON STEEL
FAT
WRECK CHORDS
IBM

data—every Big Mac eaten, every Budweiser guzzled, every Ford driven, every Winston smoked. The only Americans the Big Three corporations are concerned with now are those who can promote their products. They want glamorous Americans, beautiful Americans. So the Big Three invest in the only two industries we Americans were ever passionate about anyway: entertainment and sports. That's why hundreds of team franchises were established in the last few decades; why big budgets are granted to thousands of films. Even crappy films."

Frank paused the recording. "You bored?" he asked Angela, who was sitting in lotus position on the floor.
"No," she said.
"You sure?" he asked.
"Yeah."
He hit PLAY.

"More and more Asians are settling in America," Bittle continued, "a country they now own seventy-eight percent of. 'Here we are now—entertain us,' they say with their celestial smiles and their fat checkbooks, and Americans are only too happy to oblige. But don't believe for one second that it will be one great, big picnic! Most Americans will be unable to meet the challenges of the brave new world as, indeed, they've been unable to meet the challenges of the old one. Most of us can't play baseball well enough to make it to the pros, even in a league of two-hundred and twenty-eight teams. Neither will we all find work in show business. Educated Americans will have no place in Asian society.

As for the toothless and great unwashed, they are destined to stay that way. Non-product specifiers will be excluded from the information pool. Lower-class Americans—the fifth-, sixth-, and seventh-generation welfare recipients—will remain Non-Pro-Ducts."

"Okay," said Angela, "*Now* I'm bored. Want to make love?"

★ ★ ★

Frank was in bed watching WWF Professional Wrestling. Nick the Frothing Pit Bull had just thrown a flying wedge on Honest Abe Anderson and was about to execute an atomic knee drop when Angela walked in, an open Perdue Chicken robe partly covering her otherwise nude body.

"We've got to talk," she said to Frank, who was all but oblivious to her entrance.

"Shush! One second." Frank waved his hand.

"Frank!"

"Just a sec...just one more... Shit! I can't believe this! You *had* him, Nick!" The Pit Bull was flat on his back; Honest Abe had reversed, taken him down, covered, and held tight to the three count. The crowd was going crazy when Angela shut off the set.

"Hey!" Frank yelled, flicking it back on just as Honest Abe turned his back to the camera. *Intel Inside*, read the wrestler's back.

"I have to talk to you and you're watching this crap!"

"It's the championship," said Frank.

"You know this is all fake."

"What isn't?" he replied.

"Me!" Angela screamed. Her face reddened. "I'm not!" And then she began to cry.

"Hey!" Frank sprang to his feet. "What'd I say?"

She sobbed gently. "It's not what you *said*—it's what you *did*."

"Huh?"

"I'm pregnant, Frank."

"You're *what?*"

"Pregnant!" She looked at the floor and said it again.

Frank gaped dumbly. "Uh, uh...That's *good* news, isn't it?"

"I don't think so," said Angela. "No one hires knocked-up strippers.

– 22 –

I never planned on being a single mother, and I don't want an abortion no matter how many bonus credits the government gives me!"

"Hey, wait a minute!" said Frank, suddenly indignant and with what Angela thought a wholesome and greedy look in his eye. "Who said anything about an abortion?"

Angela took a step forward, shifting from soft and sobby to angry. "I'm *not* selling my baby, Frank!" She emphasized the point by stamping her foot.

"Who said anything about selling?" Frank moved closer to Angela, put his hands on her hips and gently pulled her toward him. "I love you, Angie. I want this baby."

"Really, Frank?"

"Really. I mean it. Let's get married right away."

A tear rolled down her cheek.

"And as for your stripping," said Frank, and he loosened her towel, which dropped to the floor, and the two made love in the middle of the Nabisco rug.

★ ★ ★

The nearest justice of the peace, who Frank found through a quick communifile search, was a proud sponsor of Pampers. According to the address posted, his office was just two sectors away, a fast five-minute ride by tram, but Angela wanted to walk. Frank resisted. Walking meant passing through a bad sector, underclass types such as refugees from the last Balkans war, or attorneys; squalid trailer parks where people were born, raised, and died early; people who never exercised; who smoked too much, drank too much, and ate bad food. Neither were they encouraged to change their consumption habits. The Big Three thought there were too many Americans to begin with.

Frank and Angela finally came upon the office building. He pressed the entrance button and a voice from an overhead speaker said, "May I help you?" The voice was neither male nor female.

"We're here to see the justice of the peace," said Frank.

"Do you have an appointment?" the voice asked.

"No," said Frank.

"That will be seventy-five credits."

Frank pulled back his sleeve and ran his wrist over the infrared scanner above the button.

"Her, too," said the voice.

Frank sighed, shook his head, and mumbled something as Angela stepped up and allowed her barcode to be scanned.

"Thank you," said the voice as the door opened.

The justice stood just inside the doorway ready to greet his blushing clients. He was a little man, the justice, and fairly old, with bad teeth and bad breath and non-designer clothes. He looked like a typical Spotless, save for the Crest Toothpaste logo on his forehead. "So you folks want to get married?" he asked. He had a big, snaggle-toothed smile.

"That's right," said Frank.

Angela nodded.

"Well," said the justice, "let's go, let's go!" He held out a black plastic pad and instructed the couple to place their hands on the touch-sensitive surface. They obliged. Then the justice punched a few buttons and looked at the readout. "Oh, well," he said. "You're incompatible. Sorry."

"We're what?" asked Frank.

"Hard of hearing?" asked the justice. "I said you're *incompatible.*

You're owned by different conglomerates." He wiped his nose on his sleeve. "'Fraid there's nothing I can do about it. Better luck next time." He turned away.

"Wait a minute!" said Frank, his voice raised. "You're saying you won't marry us?"

"Can't," said the justice. "The law is the law."

"*What* law?" asked Frank.

"The Conflict of Interest Act. Now if you don't mind…"

"I…I don't understand," said Angela. She was starting to hyperventilate.

The justice shook his head. "If you two had a sixty-percent or higher overlap, I'd marry you. But you don't. So I can't. Is *that* clear enough?" He was getting annoyed. Wanted to go back and watch the WWF Championship.

"Just hold on, mister," said Frank. "I may be dumber than I look, but something doesn't figure here. Who gives a rat's ass who I marry? Whose business is it besides mine and Angela's?"

"It's your sponsors' business, sonny," said the justice. "Your advertisers give a rat's ass, if you don't mind."

"But this is America!" Frank said. "It's a free country."

The justice smirked. "It's America, all right, but the only thing free is an abortion. Why don't you two just live together like everyone else? It's the American way."

Frank pulled Angela by the hand and the two left.

The justice stood there mumbling to himself, "Dumb kids."

★ ★ ★

"I'm removing a tat," said Frank.

"You *can't*," said Angela. Her eyes were red and puffy, but she'd finally stopped crying. "And even if you *could*, it's against the law."

"I don't care."

"Forget it, Frank. I'll just get the abortion. We can use the credits."

"No, Angie."

"You can't breach a contract, Frank!"

"To hell with them! They're not running my life!" His hands clenched in and out.

Angela put her arms around her man and massaged his back muscles to calm him down. In the ten weeks they'd been sleeping together, she'd never seen him like this. "I'm afraid, Frank," she said, her voice almost a whisper.

"Of what?"

"I don't want to lose you. I don't want you to end up..."

Frank looked down at her. "What, honey?"

"I...I don't want you to end up like your father."

Frank suddenly laughed, his mood broken. "I'm *nothing* like my father," he assured her. "My old man was a martyr. Gave up his whole life for social consciousness. What *I* do," Frank declared, "I do for love."

★ ★ ★

The orange-neon tube on the door flashed a pair of Momus and Komos. Just below the masks, the words:

TATOUAGE ARTISTIQUE
Sterile Equipment
Custom Work
Thousands of Designs

Frank had located the establishment on the Ink Fever Website. The joint had one of the highest techno ratings of any non-corporate skin-art provider. "These Teutonic artists," said the Web-crit, "enjoy a worldwide rep for outstanding skill and superior iconography."

Frank opened the door and went inside. He looked at the wall displays, the flash—everything from Japanese kabuki to Frank Frazetta. These guys were *good*.

"You know why they call it flash, don't you?"

Frank turned, found himself face-to-face with a man about a foot and some shorter than himself. The man had tiny dark eyes and a scruffy blond goatee, and his head was shaved clean to display a Sanskrit Vishnu symbol just above where his ponytail began. His body was tight and angular, not beefy like Frank's, and he wore a see-through polyurethane shirt, exposing a neck-to-waist manifold of artful, non-corporate tats. Frank's eyes darted to the man's nipples, both pierced and connected to one-another by a herringbone chain, which attached to a pair of spun-gold hoops through the apertures.

"Cause they're flashy?" Frank answered.

"Nope. Flash is an old carny expression," said the man, proud of his scholarship. "In the 1930's, flash meant anything on the midway. I'm Taz."

"Frank," said Frank, extending his hand, adding, "You're in good hands."

"You're in *better* hands," said Taz. "What can I do for you?"

Frank looked around the empty parlor as if to see if anyone was listening, then back at Taz. "I have a sort of unique request," he said.

The tattooist smiled. "Custom work's my middle name, fella. Want to see some photos?"

Frank shook his head. "What I need is really different."

"Listen," said Taz, "My specialty is pattern work, tribal, Haida, Celtic. But I can do anything. Really. Want to see some photos?"

Frank leaned closer, dropped his voice to a whisper. "I need a corp tat removed." He studied Taz's eyes for a reaction.

Taz grinned. "That's all?" he asked.

"Yup."

"Well then, *fuck you officer!*" said Taz, his voice and posture changed. "I'm no scab vendor! This is a law-abiding establishment!"

"I assure you," said Frank, "I'm not a cop."

"Well, if you *are*, this is attempt to entrap, and I can sue your faggot ass. And if you're *not*," Taz stepped into Frank's face, "get your corporate-covered derriere out of my shop!"

"You don't understand..."

"I understand just fine, shit stain," said the little man, his index finger poking Frank in the chest, backing him toward the entrance. "You've obviously never heard of Conspiracy to Breach Contract. Better luck next time, dick head."

* * *

Frank tried them all. Stig's Tatowierstudio on the boardwalk; Skin Deep Body Art in Central Jersey; Fatti Un Tatuaggio in Center City, Philadelphia...He moved on to the custom-body specialists at Graven

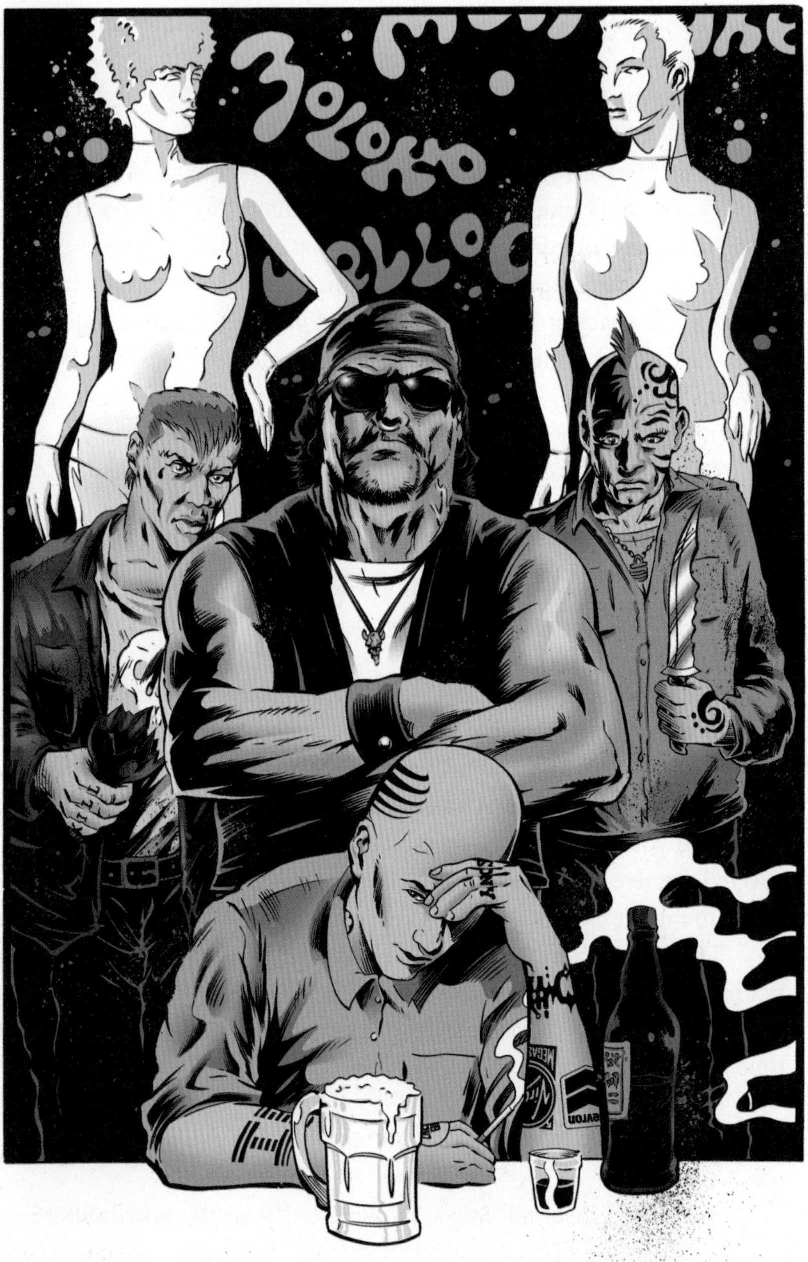
Золото

Images in Lansing, Michigan, then headed two-hundred miles south to see the old school professionals at Skinquake in Indianapolis, then west to In-The-Flesh Dermagraphic Studios in Moreno Valley, California…then he spun two-thousand miles north-east to Future Skin in Ottawa, Canada. An ill-informed lead brought him down to Sailor Moses, the famed High Practitioner of Hocus Pocus in Biloxi, Mississippi, then he headed west again to visit The Paul Rogers Tattoo Research Center in Berkeley, California. Rogers had been one of the fathers of modern tattooing—his followers were considered the most knowledgeable in the field. But it was fruitless, all of it. Frank was spending a fortune in credits on tram passes, but no one would help him.

He decided to attend the Meeting of the Marked. It was a major expense, but the thirty-fifth annual convention, held each year in Pittsburgh over the Halloween weekend, promised to put Frank in touch with hundreds of skin artists.

Ten thousand were in town for the event. The convention floor was thick with people covered in heavy ink. Frank was the only one displaying corp tats, though, which made him feel like a freak. Nevertheless, he went from booth to booth, seeking help or just information on tattoo removal. He learned that ruby-laser technology was still the state of the art for tat purging—had been for decades. Nevertheless, no one would touch him. Not for any amount of credits.

It was day three of the convention. Frank sat at the Korova Milkbar listening to the Heaven Seventeen blaring on the laser-juke, which looked like an old Wurlitzer, the tourists being keen on antique Americana. He was drinking a milk-plus, his third, which made his head as heavy as his heart. He hadn't seen Angela in weeks.

"WalMart, huh?"

Frank didn't look up. He thought he was dreaming. The milk-plus had already taken. "Talking to you, corporate tool!"

There was some rude laughter behind Frank, several voices, which shook him from his self-imposed catatonia. Dizzily, he swiveled around on his barstool, and was confronted by…Jack Nicholson?…It took Frank a moment to realize it wasn't the deceased actor but a terrific likeness tattooed on a tremendous chest, larger than life-size, at least larger than Frank-size.

"Nichol-shon," Frank slurred, the milk-plus surging through his veins.

"Whazzat?" the big man demanded. He looked like a biker, Frank thought, then amended his thought and decided the biker looked like The Thing from The Fantastic Four.

"Th-Thang," Frank slurred.

The biker-Thing with the Nicholson tattoo grabbed Frank by the scruff of his shirt and hoisted him out of the stool. "You work for WalMart, creep?"

"Huh?" asked Frank.

"I axed you if you worked for WalMart!" More laughter. It came from two smaller biker-Things standing behind the one dangling Frank in the air.

"Hey," said Frank. "There's a couple of...urp...people over there I didn't even shee before..."

"Answer me, punk!" biker-Thing demanded.

Frank shook his head, trying to clear the cobwebs. "Don't work fer n'body," he slurped.

"Then why you wear a shittin' WalMart tat on your head!"

Frank tried to answer, but the biker-Thing didn't give him a chance. "WalMart ruined my granddad's business! I fuckin *hate* WalMart!"

"Lishen up," Frank stammered. "I don' like those cocksuckersh either, 'kay? Came all the way here, all the way from Jersey, jus'... jus' to find someone to remove the tats."

The big guy lowered Frank to the floor. He cocked his head slightly. "You mean it? You really wanna remove that WalMart on the back of your noggin?"

"I...urp...I would love to," said Frank.

"No problem," said biker-Thing, grabbing Frank once again and cocking his other huge ham of a fist in the air. "I'll help you out by removing your head."

Frank didn't remember the lights going out.

★ ★ ★

"It's not worth it, Frank."

Frank's eyes opened at the sound of the voice, then squinted shut again. The bright lights hurt, but he wanted to see her, so he forced them back open, blinking in the adjustment. "I...missed...you," he said

"I missed you, too, sweetheart." Angela touched his cheek.

"Does that hurt?"

"No." The pounding in his head was the only worthy pain Frank was aware of. Perhaps, when that subsided, the broken jaw would be less comfortable, too. Everything is relative, thought Frank.

"I've made a decision. We'll have the baby and just live together."

Frank didn't answer.

"Okay, Frank?"

He closed his eyes again. "No," he said.

"Why?! Why do you insist on getting married? This is so ridiculous! You almost got killed out there! Can't you just leave well enough alone?"

"No," Frank repeated.

Angela removed her hand from his face. "You are *so* stubborn!"

"My parents," said Frank, "raised me different than that. The old man used to say the breakdown of the family is what ruined this country in the first place."

"Terrific," said Angela. "Now you're quoting your father."

"He was a wise man."

"Really? And when did you start admiring him?"

"Never stopped," said Frank. "Just didn't agree with him."

"And now you do?"

Frank paused. "Let's just say I'm starting to understand him better." He tried to sit up, winced from the pain, then tried again.

"What are you doing?"

"Have to get out of this hospital," he said.

"Why?"

"Have to see someone."

"Who?" she demanded. "You've already been across the entire country twice. No one is sticking their neck out for you. Face it, Frank—you're tattooed for life."

Frank managed to pull himself into an upright position. Painfully, he swung his feet over the bed and gently placed them in the Toyota slippers on the floor. "I know who can help me," he said. And with that, pain and all, he stood up.

★ ★ ★

The room was tiny, dark, and immaculately clean. It made Frank feel claustrophobic. He adjusted his position in the swivel chair for the fifth time and stared across the table.

"You listening?" the old man asked.

Frank leaned forward to indicate that he was.

"What you're asking for isn't simple." The old man cleared his throat, then scratched his arm, slowly, deliberately. "Gotta be careful what you say in here. Walls have ears."

Frank looked around, then nodded.

"Lots of ex-corporate vecks realize we've been conquered—that the puppet government in Washington doesn't care anymore about the welfare of citizens today than elected officials used to. There are men who can help you break your electronic chains, Frank. But know this: Once you do that, you're a runner. You're down under, boy. You get me?"

Frank nodded.

"You damn well better, because there's no turning back. Not *ever*. Once you remove—" The man looked around, then back at Frank and resumed whispering, "once you remove a corp tat, you're worthless. Worse than a non-product specifier. You're a breacher. A piece of shit."

"What if I only remove one?" asked Frank. "I can understand *that* company coming after me, but why should their competitors give a damn?"

The old man's eyes scrunched up. "Competitors? What competitors?"

Frank looked around, then whispered, "The Big Three."

"*The Big Three*," the old guy repeated sarcastically. "I used to believe that, too. But I was wrong. There's just *one*, Frank. The Big *One*."

Frank was bewildered and scratched his head to prove it. "If that's true, if there's just one company, why the farce? Why pretend there's competition?"

"Because it's not about competition," said the old man. "It's about *control*. One day the Asians woke up. They said there's five billion of us and only two-hundred million Americans. Why the hell are we trying to conquer *that* market? The *real* market is Asia. But the way to sell product to Asians is to make it *feel* American. So shortly after the last Balkans war relegated Europe back to the dark ages, the good old U.S.A. became a placard for Asian companies. The only thing an American can be today is an icon for the rest of the world, or an untouchable. Americans are the media."

Frank sat there blinking, his face fallen.

"Don't take it so hard, boy. It's no great revelation—just bondage disguised as freedom. Slavery masquerading as choice. Same as it ever was."

"I don't care about any of this!" said Frank. "I just want to know how—" He looked around again. "How do I suck this damn ink out of my skin?"

The old man scratched his arm again deliberately. "I'm trying to help you best I can."

Frank looked at his father's itchy arm and noticed the barcode. "Thought you burned that out," he said.

"I did. That's how they caught me. Traced me soon as the signal died." He scratched one more time. "Never let your right arm know what your left arm is doing."

Frank stared at his father's arm. Then, all at once, he understood.

He sighed a heavy sigh, said thanks, and got up to leave.

"By the way, Dad," he said, "I'm getting married."

* * *

Angela looked like she was about to climax when her face suddenly relaxed. Then she rolled her eyes, brushed a wisp of damp hair from her forehead, and climbed off Frank.

"What's wrong?" he asked.

"The baby's crying again."

Frank sighed, covered himself, lit a Marlboro, and lay back staring at the Trojan ad. Ten minutes later, Angela returned, hair mussed, groggy from baby-rocking. She was startled as she passed the closet.

"Please," she said, shutting the closet door. "Keep that door shut!"

Frank chuckled. "Can't believe that still spooks you. It's a just symbol of our love."

"I don't need symbols." She climbed back into bed. "Besides, the baby might crawl in there and break it. He's into everything now."

"How's he gonna break two-inch thick plexiglass?"

"He might pull a wire and screw up the signals. I don't know—but let's not take any chances. Now where were we?"

"I think you were about to come." Frank blew a smoke ring.

Angela snuggled closer. She drew little circles on Frank's abdomen.

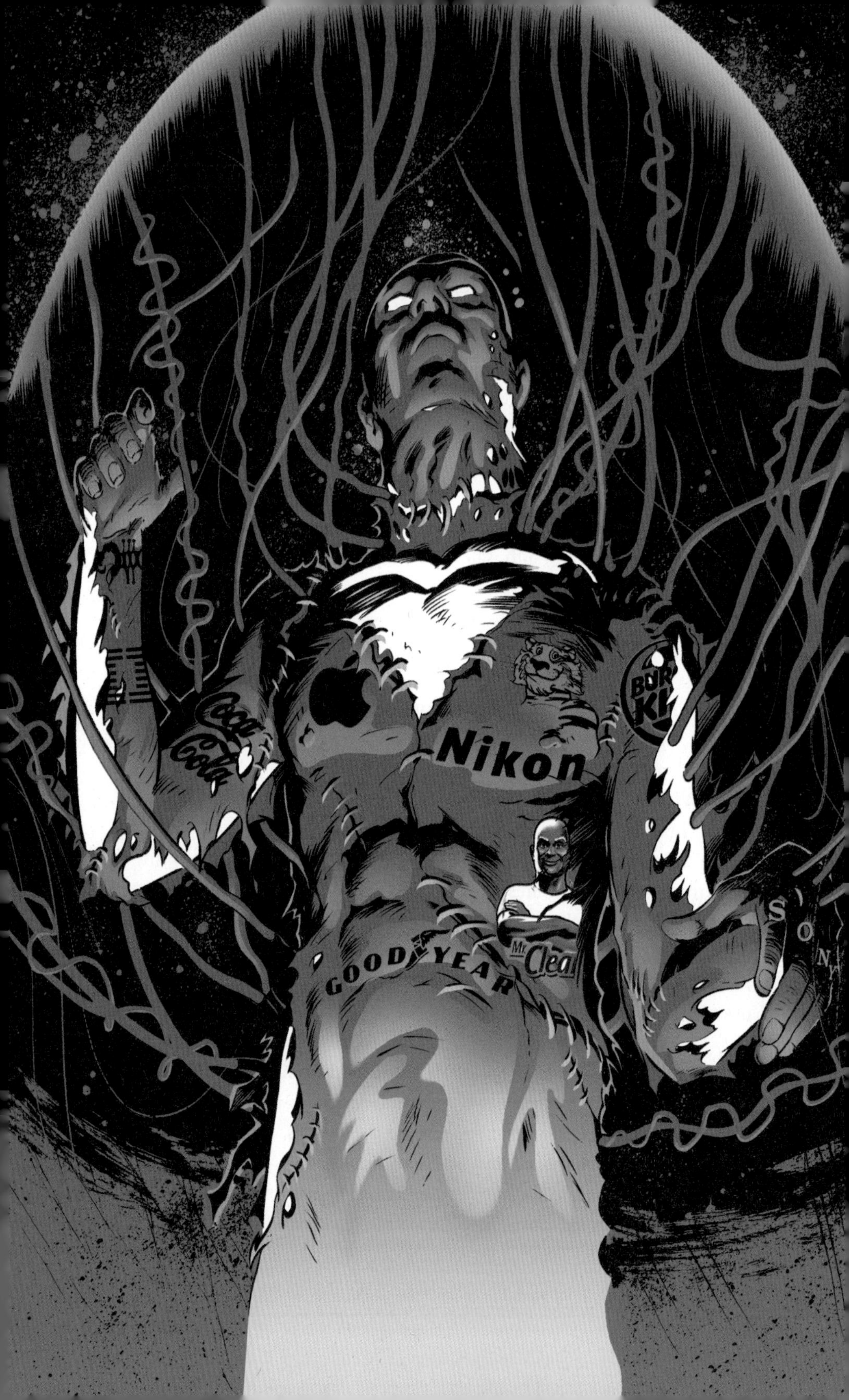

Coca Cola
Nikon
GOOD YEAR

"Does that feel good?"

"It's okay."

"I mean does it feel as good as it used to?"

"Hard to say. Can't remember what it used to feel like." He glanced at the closet. In his mind's eye, he could see his old skin stretched over the dress-store mannequin. "Reeber's thinking of getting peeled, too," he said offhandedly.

"Really'?" Angela asked. "I didn't know he wanted to get married."

"Doesn't," said Frank. "In fact, he's thinking of dumping that fat bitch Carolyn. But he's concerned about the future. Speaking of which, I need a favor." He got out of bed and stepped toward his dresser, where he spied the glass pedestal—inside, a hand was flipping the bird, its raised middle digit revealed a fluorescent-green '*R IN GOOD*. Beside the pedestal sat a wallet from which Frank pulled a business card. "Reeber's stopping by tomorrow. Give this to him, wouldja?"

"Sure." Angela looked at the card. It said:

MACHEN MENSCHEN

Artificial Limbs * Synthetic Epidermis

Three Chairs * No Waiting

"They still make these?" asked Angela.

"Bio-electronic prosthetics? Are you kidding?"

"No," said Angela. "Business cards."

"Of course," said Frank, back in bed, reaching for his wife. "It pays to advertise."

Wagging The C.E.O.

"Shit," said Jonah Zwillman.

"How high?" asked Rob Ligner.

"No," said Zwillman. "Not the verb. The expression. I think it's a noun."

Ligner was relieved. He had taken a huge crap just before this meeting and was unsure if he could move his bowels again if compelled to do so.

"What's wrong, Jonah?" he asked timidly. "You don't like the business plan?"

"No," said Zwillman. "I forgot my glasses." Zwillman looked down at a pigs-in-clover puzzle he'd borrowed from his second grader and played with it.

"Here," said Ligner. "Take my glasses." He quickly snatched a pair of horn-rimmed spectacles from the bridge of his nose and handed them to the billionaire C.E.O.

Zwillman put on the glasses and looked over the top at the people sitting around the conference table. In addition to Ligner, there were three representatives from Advanced Septic Systems. Zwillman looked at them as if he'd never seen a human being before in his life. "So let me get this straight," he said. "I get fifty-one percent of your patents, your R&D, and your government contracts—that is, if you ever secure any."

"That's correct," said a man in a crisp, dark suit named Gutnick.

"And all I have to do is give you four million dollars." Zwillman leaned back and put his Keds on the mahogany conference table.

"It's important to bare in mind," said Gutnick, "that the Environmental

Protection Agency has already shown serious interest in—"

"How about the pay-toilet rights," Zwillman interrupted.

"The what?" asked Gutnick. He was surprised by the non sequitor.

"The rights to coin boxes on all of the toilets," Zwillman said tonelessly.

"I'm afraid you misunderstood," said Gutnick. "We don't actually own the toilets. Our technology just makes it possible to—"

"I know what it does," said Zwillman. "You just spent twenty minutes telling me about it. But what I'm really interested in is the toilets. It seems to me that's where the real money is. A technology that converts crap to toothpaste is intriguing, but I think it's limited because there's only so much toothpaste that people really need and it might be distasteful to some people. But if we can put coin boxes on the toilets where the processors are installed, then I think we'll hit a homerun."

Ligner snapped to attention. "It's brilliant! I'll get our attorneys to tie-up the ancillary rights. You've done it again, Jonah!"

The three men from A.S.S. stood up and everyone around the room shook hands, except for Zwillman, who stayed seated and continued to work on the pigs-in-clover puzzle. He just couldn't seem to go all three balls in the holes at the same time; he'd get two in, but when he'd just about drop the third ball, one of the first two would pop out and roll freely again. Finally frustrated by the toy, he flung it across the table. "Shit!" he exclaimed.

"How high?" asked Ligner.

Revisions On The Pea

for Peter David

The smaller god stood motionless, his face somewhat reddened, his tongue bloating as he sought for the right words or wrong words or any words at all. But the medium god chimed in again before he could comment on the news he'd just heard.

"I'm sorry," said the medium god, "but you know how things go. Only fifteen percent of these matters ever come down to the actual *writing*—the rest is purely political."

The smaller god nodded in understanding, but his face betrayed his bewilderment, and then his words betrayed the rest of him. "Do they really expect me to start *all* over again? As in *from the beginning*? You've got to admit that's a little ridiculous at this point. I mean you're asking for a page-one rewrite after they've already approved the treatment."

"It was a *step outline*," said the medium god.

"No, it was a *treatment*," said the smaller god. "I gave you beat by beat."

The medium god snickered a little, just barely, but there it was. He wasn't large by any stretch of the hierarchy, but certainly larger than small, and echelon begets snickering. "Either way," he said a tad glib, "Rachel wants something *more*, which is not to say something entirely *else* but rather—"

"*If*," interrupted the smaller god, "Rachel and the others would red-line the first draft, and then—"

"No, no," said the medium god, returning the interruption, "Rachel isn't ready for that yet. She must see a *theme* first."

"I *gave* her a theme," said the smaller god, now up on his toes and somewhat less small, if only by a fraction. "The theme is *The Nature of Heroic Expectations Versus The Transcendent Temperament of Displeasure.*"

"That's not a *theme*," said the medium god. "It's an *arena*. Theme is something we can hang the narrative thread on. As in—" The medium god went on to define several themes. The example he preferred was: A woman has a big secret that she's keeping from her son and finally lets it slip in an awkward moment only to discover that her son has a tidy little secret of his own.

The smaller god was relieved to hear these details, even though what the medium god had put forth was *conflict*, not theme. He smiled but kept his mouth shut, as smaller gods are apt to do, at least the clever ones who want to get work. The details put forth indicated that he wasn't being replaced by another small god, which would have been easy enough, smaller gods being a dime a dozen. Medium gods were a dime a dozen, too, but they usually had an in with a *larger* god.

"Are we clicking?" asked the medium god.

"Like a cuckoo," said the smaller god as the reality poured over him. "What you're really trying to say is that Rachel and the others didn't read the script."

Slowly, the right side of the medium god's mouth curled a bit. He nodded sardonically, or at least he nodded. "No, I don't expect they did," he said. He clapped his hands together, apropos of nothing, then said, "Now don't be insulted."

"Oh, I'm not insulted. I was sort of expecting this from them."

"Were you?"

"Yes," said the smaller god, "I was just hoping they wouldn't live down to my expectations."

★ ★ ★

Further down, it was warm for mid-winter and early in the evening and inside the split-level North Jersey home it was going something like this:

"I have to finish packing tonight."

Hank looked over at his wife. Anyone at all could see he was properly annoyed. It was one hell of a time for her to be going away and all he could think of was the cooking and the cleaning and the dogs and the half-dozen other things he couldn't quite grasp. He wasn't sure how'd he'd function with her away and he made no effort to hide his displeasure.

"Aw," said his wife responding to her husband's middle-age pout. "Don't be sad. It's just a vacation." She winced suddenly, then smiled again and reached for his hand. "Quick," she said, "feel my stomach! The baby is moving."

Hank pat the hard, little bulge beneath his wife's otherwise flattish stomach. It felt like a tumor. "I don't feel anything," he said.

"Nothing?" she asked.

"Just a tumor," he said.

"It's not a tumor," she said with a laugh. "Just wait." She stared up at the ceiling.

He waited and waited some more. Still nothing.

"Oh, well," she said at last, dismissing his hand. She stretched a little, then smiled over at her husband once more. "I have to tell Skipper about the baby as soon as I return. Unless, of course, he's figured it out already. I hope he hasn't. I don't want to ruin this trip for him."

Hank sighed with transparent disgust. He knew better than to comment, but he did it anyway. Everyone does. "Why would your being pregnant *ruin* your kid's little vacation?"

"Do you always have to call him my *kid*? Can't you even say his name?"

"Aw, Jeez—"

"And why is everything about him *little*? His *little* vacation. Would you like it if I talked that way about your children?"

Hank sat up and yawned intentionally. "Okay," he said, "you win. Let's drop it."

"No," said his wife, "I don't want to just drop it—I want to *resolve* it."

"It's our last night together for two whole weeks—can we please do this some other time?"

"It's so easy for you to just blow it off!"

"We're in love, right?"

She hesitated for a second, then, "Yes, we're in love, but—"

"And we're having a baby," he said. "So let's not fight on our last night together. That'll be a helluva thing to think about for two weeks."

"Okay," she agreed.

"Two weeks," Hank repeated.

"It'll go fast," she said.

"For *you*."

"You *know* I don't want to be away from you that long," she said, "but I'm hoping this trip will help Skipper. Maybe he'll change his mind about... Or have a revelation! Wouldn't that be nice?"

"Now he's having revelations."

"Well, what better place to have a spiritual awakening than Jerusalem?"

★ ★ ★

The medium god looked up. "It's better," he said, "But I still think the Hank character is a little thin."

"I had him at about 170 lbs.," said the smaller god.

"That's not what I meant."

"Kidding," said the smaller god. "So what specifically doesn't work?"

"I'm not sure. I just don't like him."

"But you like the wife?"

"Oh, yes," said the medium god. "She's quite...likable. Realistic."

"Not too spacey?"

"I don't think so," said the medium god. "A lot of female characters are written like that. But the Hank character is just too mean."

"How so?"

"Over here," said the medium god, turning to page 46. "When his wife tells him that Skipper just got into Harvard and Hank says, 'Great. He won't have to leave the state to get married.' That's just *mean*. Rachel won't like it."

"That's how the Hank character talks."

"I don't think so. A Martian wouldn't say that."

"Okay. Fine," said the smaller god. "We'll change it."

★ ★ ★

Down below, inside the upper Eastside apartment, Skipper had just finished meticulously folding all of his clothes, then packing all of his meticulously folded clothes into his new Gucci travel bag. He preened before the mirror, first with one tie held up to his chin, then another. Then he turned around.

"So which one do *you* think I should wear?"

"The yellow and pink one," said Bruce.

Skipper looked disappointed. "You don't think the baby blue one is more appropriate?"

"Well," said Bruce, "it *does* bring out your eyes."

Skipper went back to the mirror. He turned toward his left profile, his best side, relatively speaking, and batted his eyelashes. "But you like the yellow and pink one better?"

"That's *always* been my favorite," said Bruce. "You were wearing that one when we met and I complimented it. Do you remember what you replied?"

"Yes," said Skipper. "I said, 'it's a reinterpretation of fabric and texture.'" He smiled again. He was terribly proud of himself and, as usual, in a *super* mood.

★ ★ ★

The medium god pursed his lips, shook his head and looked up.

"What's the problem, now?" asked the smaller god.

"Skipper is *way* too obvious."

"That's the point," said the smaller god.

"*What's* the point?" asked the medium god.

"That he's *obvious*. He's an archetype; so supra-conscious of the conventions that he can only navigate within the confines of ultra-stereotypical behavior."

"Rachel won't get it."

"No," said the smaller god with a sigh and a shake of his big head. "I don't suppose she would."

"We'll have to change it."

"Yes," said the smaller god, rolling his eyes. "I suppose we will."

"Now look," said the medium god, catching the tone, "Rachel has been in this job for as long as I can remember; she's read ten-*thousand* scripts…"

"Which entitles her to read ten-thousand and *one*," said the smaller god. Even *he* didn't believe he'd said that, but there it was.

"I'm sorry," said the medium god, "I don't mean to be nit-picky, but I know the coverage team. Even if you squeak a stereotype by Rachel, the policy has changed at the front office. Nothing gets green-lit if it's the least bit offensive."

"Rachel forbid!" said the smaller god.

"Are we being sarcastic again?" asked the medium god.

"Does it make a difference?" replied the smaller god.

★ ★ ★

Meanwhile, on page 89, Skipper sat next to his mother on Flight 106 out of Kennedy. Everyone around them had already received their snacks except for the two of them and a Hassidic family near the rear of the plane who had also ordered the kosher meal. The stewardess was handing out headsets to those who were willing to part with another five bucks for the privilege of hearing the movie. The $1400 round-trip didn't include the $5 headset. As the headsets were distributed, Skipper didn't see the stewardess slip a pea under his seat. He tried to watch the in-flight movie although he knew exactly what to expect; if you've seen one Spike Lee film, you've seen them all. Skipper squirmed and adjusted his seat for the fifth time in as many minutes, then buzzed the stewardess. He wanted to ask for another pillow.

His mother saw him struggling and tapped him on the shoulder, motioning him to remove his head-set. "I have some news for you," she said.

"Actually, there's something I have to tell you, too, mommy."

"There *is*?" she asked. "Go ahead."

"No," said Skipper, "you go first."

"No, you," said his mother.

"I insist," said Skipper.

"Please," she said, "I'm not sure how you're going to take my news, anyway." She was suddenly very conscious of her belly protruding beneath the airplane safety belt.

"And I'm now sure how you're going to take *my* news either," said Skipper. He adjusted his tie, the yellow and pink one, a reinterpretation of fabric and texture, then looked down the narrow aisle. "Where is that stewardess!" he insisted. He had already asked for an extra pillow and even with three, including the one he brought from home, he was still uncomfortable.

Just then, the stewardess showed up with another pillow. She even fluffed it for him. But twenty mattresses and twenty eider-down beds on top of the mattresses wouldn't have made a difference. This was how the stewardess could be certain that Skipper was a real princess.

And the pea was put in the museum where it may still be seen.

That is, if no one has stolen it.

IV

Blowing Smoke

Jonah Zwillman sat in the executive conference room eating sushi with his fingers, as unaware of his surroundings as a frog is of the bacteria in its pond. His company had announced another $90 million loss that quarter, mostly due to its businesses in the telecommunications sector, but all Zwillman had thought about all day was Timmy's Weiner.

Zwillman stuffed another piece of sushi into his mouth, chewed a little, then decided that he wasn't sure if he liked sushi anymore. It had once been his favorite food but now he considered if that hadn't been a mistake. Swallowing most of what was in his mouth, he made a note on his yellow legal pad. The note said *sushi*. He understood that, later that day, he would examine the notation, along with all the other notations on the pad representing the plethora of ideas that had jumped that morning into his well-packed head, and he would try to remember precisely what it was he'd been thinking about. So he made another note to himself on the next line of the lined pad that said *remember*. At precisely that moment, and for no particular reason, he looked up over his glasses and noticed Rob Ligner standing at the foot of the table. Ligner, a prematurely gray-haired man who had never suffered an authentically creative thought, smiled and came to attention.

"Would you like to talk about everything now, Jonah, or would you prefer I come back?"

Zwillman blinked several times. "Rob?" he asked, as if testing to see if he had the correct name, which might have been the case. "How long have you been standing here?"

Unsure of the correct answer, Ligner half-shrugged and made a funny mouth. "Not long," he finally said. To be precise, it had been 17 minutes, but Zwillman had ignored Ligner longer than that on other occasions, so *not long* was comparatively accurate. "You wanted to talk about Timmy's Weiner?"

"Yes," said Jonah, staring at his notepad once again. He spotted the line that said *Timmy's Weiner* and put a checkmark next to it. "You see, I had this idea that maybe Timmy should have a friend. Maybe the bun should also be sentient, you know, like Judy the bun, or...uhm...Betty the bun."

Ligner furrowed his brow as if thinking, pursed his lips, and nodded. "It's funny—I was thinking the same thing, but I wanted to be careful that it didn't have any sexual connotations."

"Sexual?" asked Jonah, as if he'd never heard the word pronounced correctly.

"Well, Jonah, you and I both know it's only a cute children's story with great entertainment potential, but when a salesman is pitching the concept to the buyers, we don't want there to be connotations of anything even *alluding* to sex."

"I'm not following you," said Jonah, reaching for another piece of sushi.

"All I'm saying is that a buyer who hasn't seen the art boards—and frankly, even if they *have*—well, a buyer might take offense at something as innocent as a talking hotdog if he—or worse, *she*—sees it as having sexual overtones. And a talking hotdog is one thing, but once you put it in a talking bun..."

"I don't think everybody has a dirty mind," said Zwillman, who suddenly began wondering if everyone had a dirty mind and, if that was the case, how he could patent it. He jotted *dirty mind* on his notepad, then hastened to add the word *patent* so he'd recall later on what he'd been thinking about earlier.

"Well, then I'll get right to work on a bun," said Ligner. "Betsy, you said?"

"Or Becky or... Beth... I like that. Beth Bun. I think it should have alliteration."

"Of course," said Ligner, who had no idea what alliteration meant. He had only been a TV writer for a short while and, failing that, a children's book editor slightly longer. He'd found no need to stretch his mouth to get words of that size to fit.

"You know Stan Lee used to do that," said Zwillman.

"Do what?" asked Ligner.

"Alliteration. You know like, uhm, Peter Parker was Spider-Man, and, uhm, Bruce Banner was the Hulk. He did that to help his memory and—" Zwillman stopped in mid-sentence. He was suddenly distracted by a piece of sushi stuck in his upper bicuspid. He tried to suck it out but to no avail. Soon, he grew so enraged with the little piece of stringy salmon that he began digging at his gums with a fingernail until they bled. He looked at his bloody finger. Before long, he'd forgotten all about Ligner. Eventually, he was able to pry the bit of fish from his tooth. He spit the bit into his hand and stared at it until he grew bored. When he finally looked up, Ligner was still there.

"I forgot you were here," said Zwillman.

"That's okay, Jonah—my wife does that all the time." Ligner laughed. He loved his job. He could never have gotten away with this level of incompetence anywhere else. In fact, he hadn't. Now that Zwillman was placated creatively, he was anxious to leave before the bottom line came up.

But it was too late.

"I understand that the children's division is losing money," said Zwillman.

Ligner's stomach jumped, but he quickly dived into his well-practiced lines. "Everyone I've spoken to in children's publishing says it takes at least nine years before you start really seeing profits, Jonah. We just have to hang in there and build our brand while gathering IP."

"IP?" asked Zwillman. His eyes flashed.

"Intellectual property. The names of the characters. Timmy's Weiner and Betty Buns and…"

"Oh. I thought you meant initial public offering," said Zwillman, his eyes registering neither relief nor understanding but Xanex.

"Wouldn't that be IPO?" asked Ligner.

"I thought you were abbreviating," said Zwillman. An idea came to mind but by the time he could jot down *abbreviating*, it was gone. Zwillman looked around the room, as if hoping to find the idea lurking in one of the corners. "Where were we?" he asked.

Reluctantly, Ligner said, "How it takes nine years to—"

"Oh, that's right," interrupted Zwillman. "Anyway, I'm not so worried about it. The way we're losing money right now, you'd think I'd be worried, but I'm not. I've just invested in a new business that I'm sure will bail us out. I shouldn't be talking about it but it's a great business with a lot of potential. I was thinking about how much money we'd lost in telecom and I realized that it was largely because of the, uhm, infrastructure and, uhm, the regulations and the competition lying about having better technology and better service. But I found a group of Indians in Connecticut who had this unique technology. I really shouldn't call them Indians—they don't like that. They prefer Native Americans but it takes too long to say that." He jotted down *Native Americans*. "Anyway, uhm, they have this technology for sending smoke signals that I think can be the next breakthrough in global communications, so I've bought the rights and our lawyers are working on the patents. I think it was the best $10 million I've ever spent."

"You're a genius, Jonah," said Ligner.

Zwillman looked up. "Rob?" he asked. "When did *you* get here?"

"I was just leaving," said Ligner. And with that he did.

Then Zwillman sucked at his tooth, certain that something was in there, but it was nothing. As usual.

The Other Woman

It was a sticky day in late August around mid-morning when she finally decided it was safe to come out again. I was at my desk working down a third coffee and trying to muddle through some work when the phone rang and I had the bad sense to answer it.

"It's me, " said Angel. "Can I talk to you?"

I took a second to catch my breath. "Okay, " I said. "You're talking to me."

"I need to see you today," she said. It was as if no time had passed—as if that cruel winter and that terribly lonely spring had just blown right by. *I need to see you. Today.* Just like that.

"Can't do it," I said. I wasn't a fool. Or maybe I was. "Have to work," I said.

"Just for a *little* while?" she pleaded. She was good, she was smooth. Just a *little* while. What's a *little* while between friends? A small, tiny while. As if March hadn't come in like a lion and devoured my lamb.

It had been three months since my wife left, just walked out without looking back. Three months. Ninety terribly lonely nights, mostly sleepless. I mean, I could *fall* asleep—just couldn't *stay* there. Lying down at midnight meant getting up at 3:00 a.m. to stare at cracks in the ceiling. Alone if you didn't count the spiders. Three months. Ninety nights. No contact from the wife and I wasn't expecting any. That relationship was deader than dead. But I hadn't heard from the angel either, not in three *years*. That was a tough pill to swallow. I'd resolved that I'd heard the last of her and just as well—knew instinctively that seeing her again now was a mistake. I'd just started to sleep again, to breathe and to eat.

"Please?" she asked.

"Okay," I said.

We made plans to meet that afternoon. The minute we hung up, I had to look for a hole to be sick in. She was coming in from Brooklyn. We agreed to rendezvous at a filling station near my office.

I had time for lunch but no stomach for it, but I ate a little anyway. American cheese on white bread. Seemed I'd been eating American cheese on white bread most of life, but I was eating less of everything now. When I was healthy, I followed the cheese sandwich with Devil Dogs or Ring Dings or Hostess Shitcakes or a huge bag of greasy chips, washed it down with a beer or two beers, but these days I ate very little and drank slightly more. I'd finally stopped losing weight but was terribly thin. Ate just enough to stay warm and keep alive, though I had no desire to live. No desire to die, either. No desire for anything and no appetite to speak of. Just cravings. Mostly, I craved love, the feeling of being accepted by God's again in the guise of a woman's affection. It didn't have to make sense. It was primal.

After that sandwich, I drove to my apartment to straighten up. There wasn't much to do. I'd left most everything I owned, except some clothes and some books, in my ex-house. Didn't care about any of it anymore. Didn't need a house and lawn. An apartment made more sense.

I walked up one flight, opened my door and looked around. Then I went to the bathroom and pissed and brushed my teeth and changed my shirt. The smock I'd been wearing smelled like a rodeo. Just the *thought* of seeing Angel again made me nervous. Then I drove to the gas station.

Before I even pulled in, I caught a glimpse of her from the road. She was wearing a white summer dress, short and daring, with a midriff cut just below her breasts. She stood next to one of the pumps talking to a young truck driver. No surprise there. I pulled up and rolled down my window.

"Get in."

She grinned, said goodbye to the truck driver, then slid in next to me. I didn't look at his eyes but I knew what they were seeing.

"Hot day," she said. Three years later. Hot day. I pulled up at a traffic light and turned to look her over for the first time. She looked good. She always looked good. Her body was still emaciated, still heroine chic, and her hair was long and flowing, like some terrifying river of quicksand. She was 23 now. Everything about her was ripe. And the madness, that was right behind her eyes.

Ten minutes later, we parked and took the one flight up to my apartment. We sat on the small couch, the only piece of furniture in the entire room. My arm was around her back, which just seemed natural. She told me how much she'd changed, how much she'd grown.

"I'm in my last year of college," she said. "You gave me that. You inspired me to study."

"At least I gave you *some*thing," I said. Meaningless. Empty talk.

"I'm getting straight A's," she said. "4.0 average. I'm the only one with the key to the Psych Lab."

I've always said it: Show me a shrink who doesn't need a shrink.

"And I'm bartending at night. Did I tell you that? I *love* it. I get a *lot* of attention. Everyone tells me I should get married and have babies and live happily ever after. But I don't believe in happily ever after. Every married guy I've ever known has come onto me."

I looked at my watch. "Is this what you came to tell me after three years?"

She leaned forward, put her small hand on my chest. "I'm in love," she said. "I'm in love with two people."

I smiled. "Sounds like your type."

"Stop it, Hank! I'm serious."

"Okay. Tell me about them."

She sat back a little, straightened her dress. "Well, one of them is Mark, who I live with. He's a cop. He has three kids from his first marriage. He's wonderful. He adores me."

"Okay."

"And the other one is you."

She really looked good. Great legs, tan, flat little tummy. But she was still nuts. And she was about to prove it.

"I killed you, Hank."

There it was.

"You *killed* me," I repeated.

"Yes. I killed you. You're dead."

"That explains it," I said. "I haven't been feeling myself lately."

"SHUTUP AND LISTEN TO ME!" she yelled. She leaped from the couch and almost stumbled. Then she stood over me in her little white dress and her machine tan with her supple wrists on her tiny waist and screamed bloody murder. "I *have* to tell you this! I *have* to be free of you! It's taken me *so* long to get up the courage to do this, now let me finish!"

I shrugged. "Fire at will," I said.

"I'm not here to *hurt* you, Hank," she said. "I *killed* you. You're dead. Do you understand?"

I nodded. "I'm dead."

"That's right."

This was the future of psychology.

"Stop looking at your watch!"

"I'm sorry," I said.

Her mad eyes darted about the room. Christ, she was pretty. She stood there looking like she was wrestling with the centuries, trying to find the right words to explain some heavy thesis she'd been formulating, but it was nowhere to be found.

"Tell me you love me!" she suddenly demanded.

I reached out and put my hand on her knee. She slapped it off.

"Tell me you *love* me!" she demanded. "*Say* it!"

"Okay, okay," I said. "I love you."

"You do?"

"Yeah," I said. "Sure. I love you. Now let's get the hell out of here." I attempted to get up from the couch, but she grabbed my shoulders and pushed me back down. Then she began to mount me.

"I've changed!" she said. "I'm not a little girl anymore!"

"No kidding," I said. Her little white dress was up around her waist.

"Do you know that I was with a woman once? Well, not just *once*. I'd done it before in my head *hundreds* of times. It was *fantastic*. I'd given up on men—given up trying to replace you."

"I was dead," I said.

"You're still dead."

"Right."

And then she kissed me hard, with fire and rage. The kiss went on and on and I finally began to relax when she pulled back and slapped me hard across the face. Then she started to cry. I held her while she sobbed. Told

– 59 –

her everything was all right, that she wasn't alone and I knew how she felt, the poor, mad little thing.

After several moments, she looked up at me through dry tears. "You *owe* me," she said.

"I owe you?"

"Tell me it again—tell me you love me."

"I love you," I said. I'd have said *anything*. I just wanted this to be over. She'd always been a little nuts and now she was over the top. I could see it in her hair. The rage, the hate—centuries old. It was hard to believe I'd once fucked up my marriage with this.

"Tell me again!" she screamed. "Say it! You're so stingy with it!"

"Angel, I *love* you. Now let's get the *hell* out of here."

"And you'll *always* love me, right? Tell me you'll *always* love me."

When I let her out of the car at the gas station, she was still saying it. As I pulled away, I could still hear the words in my head. I hear them now. I prayed it would be at least another three years before either of us were stupid enough to track the other down again.

Great body. Great legs. But nuts. Bugfuck. Certifiable.

Hank Is Having
A Mid-life Crisis
(And Everyone's Invited)

Hank answered the phone without looking at the caller I.D., which is never a good idea and he knew that, but who listens to sense? "Yeah?" he barked.

"Hank?" asked a female voice that ranged somewhere between pucelage and menopause.

"Who's this?"

"It's Deanne. How are you?"

"Who?"

"Deanne Weenie. I wrote you several letters. I'm a big fan of yours. I've read *all* of your books. Don't you remember? You finally wrote back about two years ago and asked me for a picture and I sent it to you. I have medium-length blonde hair, blue eyes, I'm 5'3", about 120 lbs. When I wrote to you, I told you about how I named my first son Ian after Ian Anderson and how my first husband left me when Ian was just two and that the guy I lived with for seven years left me and—"

"Why are you calling me?"

"I just want to talk to you because you're so smart."

"Not smart enough to unlist my number."

"Oh, I hope I'm not calling at a bad time!"

"What do you want?"

"I just want to talk to you. I love your stories so much, especially that one about the crippled guy who could make women have orgasms just by thinking about them."

"I see."

"That was a great story. There's a great picture of you on the back of your last book. I love that picture."

"Ok, ok. What are you wearing?"

"Right now?"

"No, last Wednesday."

"Last Wednesday? I don't remember what I was wearing, but I can try to figure it out if you want me to..."

"Jesus."

"What?"

"What the fuck are you wearing *now*?"

"Now? Oh, uh—let me see... black men's socks and green sweat pants and a red pullover sweatshirt. I'm still in my work clothes. I work at the bottling factory and I just got home from work. I broke up with Kurt last week because I thought we were going to get married but his daughter and I didn't get along and he chose his daughter over me. I guess I can understand that but now all he wants to do is come over at night when I'm drunk and fuck me, excuse my language, but I'm not going to do that anymore because he didn't even give me a ring and we were together since last Christmas and now he's choosing her over me so—"

"Listen: If you don't shut the fuck up I'm hanging up."

"Oh, I'm sorry. Am I babbling? I always babble when I'm drunk or nervous and I'm nervous talking to you because you're the only famous person I really know and you're so smart and—"

"You've got to shut up, kid."

"Oh, I'm sorry."

"Fine. Now just sit down."

"Okay. I'm sitting down now."

"What did you say your name was?"

"Deanne."

"Now listen carefully: Don't talk. Don't say a single word unless I ask you a question"

"Okay."

"Take off your pants, Deanne."

"Ok, they're off."

"Don't talk. Just obey my voice."

"Are you going to brainwash me?"

"Jesus Murphy—I'm not going to brainwash you!"

"Okay."

"Now put your hand on your stomach."

"It's already is on my stomach."

"I said *don't talk!*"

"Okay, but you're being very controlling."

"This is your last chance before I hang up."

"Okay, I'm sorry."

"Now reach under your shirt and gently stroke your stomach with your fingertips."

"I don't have fingertips."

"Excuse me?"

"I bite my nails."

"I can't fucking believe this. Just lightly stroke your stomach, for chrisakes."

"Okay."

"And stop talking!"

"But you asked me a question!"

"Close your eyes and listen to the sound of my voice. You're relaxing. You're very relaxed. Listen to my voice. You're very, very relaxed… Now move your hand to your leg and gently stroke your inner thigh. Gently, gently… That's it. It feels good. You're getting turned on. Now put it on your other thigh."

"Uh, Hank, I really don't want phone sex."

"Are you fucking kidding me? "

"No, really. I just want to talk to you because you're so smart. I've read all your books. You're the smartest person I know. I've been with six different guys since New Years and I don't even remember having sex with some of them. They smile at me and wink the next morning and I figure I must have slept with them. If you want to make me come, you'll have to do it in person. I just wanted to call you and talk to you because I've read all of your books and you're so smart. You're the smartest person I know."

"If I was smart I'd have hung up five minutes ago," said Hank. And with that, he did. But he still felt like an idiot.

Queers

Right is not founded in opinion,
but in nature.
—*Cicero*

They called Craig Chinaski a name before they beat him, a vicious name that betrayed the reason for their attack, as if reason were a reason. The name was insignificant, its etymology obscured by social progress, progress in medicine, weather predictions, sanitation disposal, telecommunications, animal rights. Everything had marched efficiently forward since the arcane word first gained entry as a pejorative. Everything, that is, except people armed with the truncheon of moral imperatives.

Queer. They'd called him a queer.

And then they'd beaten him without mercy, about the eyes, the mouth, the ears; across the back where they tore off his shirt and tore into him with belts and switches; about the genitals and the buttocks.

Craig only spent two days in the hospital before he was released. And he'd recovered well, all things considered. But he'd never forgotten. Not after two years in his new home and new community and a new school far from the incident. His mothers had taken different jobs and moved Craig and his younger sister out of the city and into a quiet suburb. Craig was a senior at Nixon High now, looking forward to graduation, to putting his teen years behind him. But the scars were still there, the ones in his mind as genuine as those on his back. That's what kept him in check, silent and cautious while his heart ached.

Just ignore it, he thought. Ignore the feelings and they'll go away. But it didn't work. The feelings grew stronger each day. Especially at school, where the danger of being discovered was greatest.

Discovered! He knew the price of that mistake, relived the beating every time it crossed his mind—

Discovered! No! He couldn't let on how he felt. He refused to go through another beating. But his heart was pounding.

It is my heart, he told himself. *I'm not thinking with my prick, am I?* The point was moot—it was his eyes that were ultimately guilty, his eyes that wouldn't heed the lesson of history and accept the logic of social norms.

Craig felt the pulse in his throat. He had never wanted anyone so badly in his life. And it only made it worse here, as they sat so close together in class—Advanced Political Correctness: From Emily Bronte to Marlo Thomas.

He tried to avert his eyes, but they had already dismissed the lecture that Mrs. Mechanic was delivering for the eighteenth time in as many years. Her nattering was an inane drone, like a foreign-language radio program somewhere in the distance. He looked up, off to his right, and once again his eyes fell upon the object of his desire. He held the image for long moments—far longer than he knew was safe.

She was exquisite. Her name was Alynn Schleifer. She was a senior like Craig and, like Craig, a relative stranger in this strange school. Her family had moved in six weeks prior from Ontario where she'd been raised. Alynn had adjusted easily, made new friends, was already excelling in her schoolwork. She was very bright. She wanted to be a genegineer like her grandfather, Dr. Jordon Schleifer, the world-renown eugenics expert.

Alynn was also extraordinarily attractive. She had great dark eyes that were wild and mischievous, and long raven-black hair brushed back; her face was fragile porcelain with delicate features, almost oriental. At her last high school she had been a gymnast; she was slim and strong, with fine breasts and a flat stomach that she proudly kept bare.

All the girls wanted Alynn. There was something about her, an attraction beyond the natural beauty and grace. There was command. That was the only word for it. As a result, the full package intimidated the average school girl, and few had the temerity to approach her.

When the class bell rang, everyone poured into the halls. Craig watched Alynn walk toward a small group of guys and girls—an attractive, popular crowd of athletes posing and preening. Everyone greeted her. There were big smiles all around. Craig stood back, virtually invisible, watching the scene until someone tapped him on the shoulder and he turned.

"Hi, Craig!"

"Uh...hi."

"Remember me?"

"Not really." It was a lie. His name was Jack something—Shovel or Shiksel or—

"Jack Shandle. We met at Bob Milne's party."

"Oh, right, right." Craig remembered him all right. How could he forget? Jack Shandle. Football jock. Not a stuck-on-himself jock—more of a bench jockey, bare of intellect, but sly; the kind who'd get by in life on corporate politics, bluff and bluster, buttering up superiors, giving head. Sure Craig remembered him. Jack Shandle had hit on him all night long at that party until Craig finally excused himself, said he wasn't feeling well. Jack offered to walk him home—practically insisted, but Craig had slipped away.

Jack played some light ruse about not understanding the lecture, then cut to the chase. "You know the prom is coming up next week, and I was thinking, if you're not already going with somebody—"

"No!" said Craig. He didn't intend to say it so fervently, but he hadn't mastered the art of turning guys down. Nevertheless, the last thing he wanted was to raise suspicions. "I mean, no—I'm not going with anyone, yet." Craig smiled. "But I think my moms are planning a trip that weekend."

"You have two moms?" asked Jack. "That's cool. I only have one dad. He's divorced. Never see my other dad. They really hate each other. I always thought it would be cool to have two moms."

"It's okay, I guess," said Craig. "Sometimes it's crazy. You know what they say: Two periods are worse than one."

Jack laughed. His eyes twinkled.

Craig got nervous and looked at his watch. "Hey, I've gotta run to class. Thanks again for asking me."

"Well, let's get together sometime," said Jack, putting his hand on Craig's shoulder. Craig smiled, said see ya, turned to walk away, but paused when he felt a hand on his buttocks, then fingers in his rear pocket. "It's my phone number," said Jack. "Call me!"

★ ★ ★

"How was school?" Craig's mother kissed her son's cheek. She watched him toss his books on the kitchen table and fall into a chair, face in hands. "That bad, huh?"

"That bad, Amanda." He sank lower in the chair. "This guy asked me to the prom."

"Is he cute?"

"Who cares?"

Amanda approached him, put her hands on his shoulder, massaged the tense muscles in his neck. "No one said you have to go, sweetheart. If you're not ready for this—"

"He's ready, alright."

Craig looked up to see Johnna, his other mother. The huge woman entered, went straight to the refrigerator, removed a can of beer, and cracked it open.

Amanda whispered to Craig, "I think you'd better leave," and he obeyed. After a moment, she said to her wife, "That wasn't necessary."

"Just keep coddling him and see what happens."

"He's different, Johnna."

"He's not *different*. He's sick!"

"Shhh," she whispered. "He'll hear you!"

"Maybe he *should* hear me. Something's wrong with him, and he needs help. But you're still in denial—still think he's your nursing infant. No wonder he's afraid of guys."

"Stop it!"

Johnna gulped the rest of her beer, belched, wiped her mouth on her sleeve. She was a large, buxom woman, a head taller than Amanda. She put her beer can down on the counter. "Listen, hon—down at the lab, we don't even let heterosexual genes slip through anymore. We get them right at the biophore stage."

"You told me this months ago."

"Well, what I *didn't* tell you is we've made tremendous strides in bio-re-engineering. You should read the article in this week's *Time*. Anyway, there's a genegineer back at the lab who can—"

"No, Johnna! You're not screwing around with my son!" Amanda grew red in the face, her eyes swelled with tears.

Johnna moved forward and reached for her wife. "Come on, Mandy—

he's my son, too." She dried one of Amanda's tears with her thumb. "I wouldn't let anyone hurt him, would I?"

Amanda shook her head feebly. Another tear fell, splashing upon the table.

"It's okay, baby. It's all right…" Johnna took Amanda's chin, brought her lips to her wife's mouth, tasted the salty tears. Then, after a moment, "You trust me, don't you, baby?"

Amanda nodded.

Johnna released her grip. "Okay—let's talk about it later." She sat down at the kitchen table. "By the way," she said, "the house looks terrific. And dinner smells great. Get me another beer, willya?"

★ ★ ★

Craig lay back on his bed ruminating, eyes closed, his stereo blasting "Strange Days." It was his favorite disc. He imagined he was Jim Morrison strutting on stage, eyeing rabid females in the audience, that's right baby, I *am* a Sagittarius, the most philosophical of the signs—Suddenly, his door flew open. He looked up to find Phoebe in the doorway.

"Don't you ever knock?" he asked.

"I like to surprise you. Thought I'd catch you jerking off again."

Craig smirked at his little sister, who wasn't little anymore. The sixteen-year-old had developed into quite a package and she knew it and flaunted it as well as any sixteen-year-old—micro-mini skirts, push-up bra, low neck line, bare tummy. The braces ruined the image. Almost.

"When are you getting some new tunes? Like grow up already."

"Jim rules."

"Yeah, right." Phoebe snapped her gum. "King of the Queeros."

"Shut up!"

"Ooo! Touchy, touchy." She wagged her finger. "Just do me a favor and turn it down—my friends will be here any minute and I don't want them to know what a nerdo you are." She watched Craig reach toward the stereo and lower the volume. "So," she said, "Jack Shandle asked you to the prom."

Craig looked up. "Who told you that?"

She snapped her gum. "I have my sources." She played with a pencil on his dresser, caught a glimpse of herself in the mirror and pouted her lips.

"Going?"

"No."

"Oh. Not good enough for you?"

"I didn't say that."

Phoebe turned from the mirror, twirled her gum with her finger, pulled it out long and green, then snapped it back into her mouth. "Well, I'll let you know how it went."

"*You're* going?"

"Sure."

"But you're just a freshman."

"But a senior asked me, stink breath. You might have seen her. New girl. Really hot. Like I couldn't believe she asked me. Too cool. Can't wait to get in her pants."

Craig said nothing.

"It's got a nice ring to it, don'tcha think? Phoebe and Alynn."

★ ★ ★

The next day was hell. Classes dragged, especially Poli-Correct. Craig couldn't stop fidgeting, which Mrs. Mechanic noticed and brought attention to in the middle of the slide presentation—insisted that Craig sit still. Everyone laughed. He didn't have the courage to look at Alynn, but he was certain he heard her laughing, too.

Finally, after the longest 45 minutes he could remember, the bell sounded. For a change, Craig wasn't the last one out the door. He spotted the back of the varsity jacket he sought.

"Jack?"

Jack Shandle stopped. "Hi, Craig. Jeez, how embarrassing was that, huh? Dr. Mechanic—what an asshole, huh?"

"Listen, about the prom, if you haven't made other plans—"

"No, nothing." Jack smiled, eyes twinkling.

"Good," said Craig, "cause I'd really like to go with you."

"Great!" said Jack. "I'll pick you up at 7:00."

"It starts that early?"

"No. At 8:00. But I thought you might want to smoke a joint or have a beer and hang out."

"I don't smoke."

"Oh, well I don't really either. 7:15?"

"Great."

"Great."

★ ★ ★

Craig paced the length of his living room. He looked at his watch. 7:07. It had been one minute since he last looked. His date would be there in eight minutes. He wanted to throw up.

"And don't you look nice!" said Amanda. She clapped her hands together at the sight of her son in a tuxedo. "I'm so excited for you! Now don't you dare leave until I get a picture of you and Jake."

"*Jack*, Mom."

"Jack."

"I'd rather you didn't take any pictures."

"Well *I* want a picture with Alynn," said Phoebe. "Just wait till you see her, Mom. She is too dreamy! Like totally."

Craig's stomach jumped. It was the only reason he was going, just to be near her, to see her, perhaps talk to her—He shook off the thought, forced himself back to his sister. Phoebe was wearing a tight, white, thigh-length dress, backless, spaghetti straps, no bra, no stockings, no panties either he suspected. In his mind, he could see her with Alynn, drifting together, laughing, dancing, lost in each other's eyes, whispering secrets, nuzzling, his sister's hands roaming carelessly over Alynn's back, her buttocks, Alynn's over hers, the two together, entranced, alone in the universe, everyone else a backdrop, whispering in each other's ears, sneaking outside for a walk in the woods, hands clasped, running together, chasing each other playfully, stopping suddenly, breathless, hearts pounding, embracing, deeply, passionately, aflame, Alynn's hands on his sister's back, her waist, her bare thighs—

"Aren't you going to answer the door?"

Craig was startled back to reality, his palms sweating.

"I said the *door*, lame brain. I know it's not Alynn. She's not picking me up 'til quarter to eight."

"Right," said Craig. The door. His date. It was the furthest thing from his mind, but he moved toward the foyer, opened the door, and saw Jack Shandle standing there in a powder blue tuxedo.

"Hey!" said Jack.

"Hey," said Craig.

"You look terrific!" Jack leaned forward for a kiss, but Craig turned his cheek. Then Jack noticed Amanda in the living room, raised his eyebrows, whispered an apology to Craig,

"So very nice to meet you, Jake," Amanda said.

"Jack."

"Sorry. I don't know why I keep doing that."

"S'okay. People make that mistake all the time." Jack turned to Craig. "This is for you." He held out a blue and white corsage, which matched his own.

"Thanks," said Craig.

Jack's eyes twinkled. He looked at his watch. "We should get going."

"Oh, you must stay for a picture," said Amanda reaching for her camera. "Besides, the prom doesn't start until 8:00. What's the hurry?"

"No problem," said Jack. He stood next to Craig and took a deep breath to make his chest swell out.

"Get closer," said Amanda peeking through her camera's viewer.

Jack draped his strong arm around Craig and pulled him close.

"Smile," said Amanda. The flash went off. "That wasn't a smile, Craig. You can do better than that. Now I want each of you handsome young gentlemen to think of something that will make you really happy. Okay? Ready?" She snapped another two pictures. If she could have gazed into her son's mind, Amanda would have been surprised to see Alynn with her hair pulled back and wearing a yellow sweater and blue-jean skirt, just the way she looked the first time Craig saw her.

If she could have looked into Jack's mind, she would have seen her son going down on the football player.

* * *

The prom was everything Craig expected—posh, prim and proper, brimming with the entire senior class and their dates. Some of the long-time couples were wearing matching tuxes or dresses, hoping to be chosen as Prom Queens.

Crowds made Craig nervous. He looked for somewhere to retreat, but there was nothing, no corner unoccupied. He felt cold, out of place, and he was instantly sorry that he'd come as he gazed at the couples on the dance floor, slow dancing, whispering, everyone crowded together. His eyes followed the arc of the dance floor until, by chance, he spotted Alynn.

She looked better than he'd ever imagined, an ankle-length, lavender gown flowing about her like a rivulet, making her every move seem regal. By contrast, her hair was pulled back in a matching ribbon, affecting an innocent appearance. Not a queen but a princess. Next to her stood Phoebe, who looked juvenile by comparison, her back partially turned as she chatted with a football player astray from his date. Craig held his breath as he watched Alynn, screwed his courage to the sticking place, turned to Jack and excused himself, then got up from his table, took a deep breath, and walked across the dance floor, a stranger through a strange land, but heading toward the light. He approached his sister boldly if cautiously, armed with painted smile.

"Hi, Phoebes."

Phoebe looked up. "Oh. It's just *you.*"

"Having fun?"

"Like there's a meaningful question."

"Won't you introduce me to your date?"

She shook her head at him, sighed, then put her hand on Alynn's shoulder and whispered something in her ear. Alynn turned around, smiled.

"Nice to meet you," said Craig. "I'm in your class."

"So is everyone else here," she said. "Class of '28."

"I meant—"

"I know," she smiled. Perfect teeth. "I was just teasing. Poli-Correct. So what do you think of Mrs. Mechanic?"

"Hate her," said Craig.

"Me, too."

They both laughed and Craig felt something, then felt himself blush. He tried to think of something to say, but she beat him to it.

"So how do you think you did on the last test?"

"Uh, I think I did okay," said Craig. "You?"

"Awful," said Alynn. "I'm terrible at memorizing names and junk. And essays. Yuck."

"So what do you like?"

She smiled.

That was twice he'd felt it. He could sense Phoebe growing impatient.

Alynn inched toward him. "So, do you have a partner for the final project?" she asked.

"I almost forgot all about that!" said Craig.

"Me, too. I haven't even started it yet. Why don't you call me over the weekend and we can knock it off together."

"That would be perfect!" Craig's heart was pounding. This couldn't mean what she was implying. It just *couldn't*. The world didn't work like that. At least not for him. The universe had conspired against him, given him an unnatural attraction to the opposite sex. Alynn was just being friendly, that was all. She had lots of male friends—he'd seen them. He knew it would be torture spending that kind of time with her, feeling what he felt for her—but it was worth it. Besides, he'd been tortured before.

"Listen," he said, "I've got to get back, but let me give you my phone number—"

"She has our number, nerdo!" said Phoebe, rolling her eyes.

"I almost forgot!" said Alynn. "I'm going to my Uncle's house in Ontario for the weekend. Let me give you the number there and we'll do it over the phone." She fumbled in her handbag for a pen.

Craig's heart dropped. Ontario. For the weekend.

Alynn produced a pen, lifted the place card from the table and jotted something on it, then folded it and pressed it into his palm.

Craig made his way across the dance floor, clutching the folded place card like a precious pearl, his hand tingling from her touch. Back at his own table, he sat down and noticed the meal in front of him, roast chicken, and suddenly found that he had an appetite, but not for rubber chicken. His heart was still pounding. He'd talked to her. After all these weeks. And she'd smiled! At him! *For* him! A beautiful smile… And he was going to talk to her again. He could hardly believe it. Craig lifted the folded card to his nose, breathed in its fragrance, touched it to his lips, then slipped it into his shirt pocket. He was the only one currently at his table—everyone else was off dancing or outside smoking joints and cigarettes. He picked up his fork, poked at his chicken, but couldn't bring himself to take a bite.

He looked around, then glanced back in her direction, but she was gone. So was Phoebe. Craig's imagination began to run wild again. He reached into his pocket and withdrew the card, wishing to see her number, see that it was real, gaze upon her handwriting, hold the card she'd written on, handled. He unfolded it. But it wasn't her phone number. It was a note.

Meet me behind the bleachers at Ten o'clock.

He read it again. Then a third time. He folded it, put it back in his pocket, felt the pulse in his neck, immediately withdrew it and read it again. There was no mistake. He jumped suddenly at the hand on his shoulder— squeezed his hand tight over the card as he looked up.

"We haven't even danced yet," said Jack. His hand was extended.

Craig looked at Jack's hand, then at his own watch. 9:40. He was grateful Jack was there. He had twenty minutes to kill.

★ ★ ★

At 9:58, Craig excused himself to the men's room, but he didn't go there and hoped Jack wouldn't look for him. The men's room was a notorious make-out spot. Few guys went there to take a crap.

He found the exit and looked around to ensure no one was watching, then dashed outdoors into the chill night air. Behind the bleachers. It was about a three-minute walk. He ran.

Craig was out of breath when he reached the bleachers. He looked around. There was no sign of Alynn. He looked at his watch. 10:01. He pulled out the note to confirm the time, read it twice, then returned it to his pocket and looked at his watch. 10:02. He couldn't have missed her—

"Craig?"

He turned.

"Alynn, I…I…"

"It's okay. Calm down." She reached out, took his forearm in her hand.

"Alynn?" He laughed, suddenly. "You don't know how bad I've wanted to say your name—just say it out loud."

"I *do* know." She smiled, tossed her hair.

"Alynn. I just—I can't believe this."

"I knew it. I believed it."

"This can't be happening. I'm dreaming. This can't be true."

"I knew it would happen like this."

"But how could you know?"

"The way you look at me. The way I feel. You're not like them."

"Alynn—"

"Oh, Craig."

They held each other for long moments. She was braver than he. He was the first to break away. "I've got to get back," he said.

"Don't."

"I don't want to."

"I know."

"But—"

"It's okay. I understand."

"I really don't want to leave you, but if I don't get back before someone notices—" The thought frightened him.

"Are you alright?"

He smiled. "The way you say that. My God! It's as if—"

"As if I've known you all my life." She smiled, held his hands, kissed his knuckles, allowing her lips to linger. "I understand," she whispered.

He looked at his watch again. "I have to go."

"I know."

"When can I see you again?" he asked.

"Anytime you want to."

"Tomorrow night. Here. Same time."

She nodded. "I'll be here."

Craig smiled at her, hugged her, then ran back to the prom.

★ ★ ★

Jack Shandle pulled over to the side of the road and cut the engine, then killed his headlights. It was suddenly very dark.

"Where are we?" Craig asked. He looked around. There were no houses in sight, only woods.

Jack smiled. "A secret detour." He put his strong arm on top of the car seat, placed his hand behind Craig's head. "I thought we could get to know each other a little better."

"I'm really tired, Jack," said Craig. "I just want to get home." Craig looked straight ahead through the windshield toward the road, which was barely visible, lit only by a sliver of a moon. He carefully avoided Jack's eyes.

"You know," said Jack, "these prom tickets cost me a lot of money, to say nothing of this tux. I have a really special evening planned for us."

"I had a great time," said Craig. "I really appreciated you asking me, but I think I drank too much and I don't feel so great—"

Craig's stomach jumped when he felt the hand on his knee. His heart began to pound. "Why don't I call you? Tomorrow—" The hand was moving, slowly but with clear intention. It was on his thigh now. He covered it with his own hand, blocked it from going any further. Then Jack's other hand, the one around his back, pulled him closer. "Really, Jack, I'm just not—"

Jack leaned over to kiss him, but Craig sharply turned away.

"Please—"

"I really like you Craig. From the first time I saw you at Bob's party—"

"I can't do this, Jack. I don't—" He felt the hand again, this time on his belt buckle. "Jack, I—" The hand was moving, the buckle was unfastened, now the hand was working his zipper—

"Oww!" Jack fell back in his seat holding his eye, which smarted and teared. "What the fuck is wrong with you? Why did you hit me?"

"Just take me home," said Craig.

★ ★ ★

Craig didn't hear Phoebe enter his room. His eyes were closed and he was playing The Doors louder than usual, singing soulfully, "Let's swim to the moon; let's fly to the tide—"

"I guess *some*one had a good time tonight."

Craig didn't bother to open his eyes—he just continued to sing.

Phoebe walked over to the stereo, lowered the music, then said, "Aren't you going to ask me why I'm back so early?"

Craig stopped singing and looked up at her. "Did it ever occur to you that I might not be interested in you bursting in here?"

"I'm back," she continued, "because my date ditched me."

"What a surprise."

"Ditched me for another girl. Like how embarrassing is that?"

Craig looked surprised. "Another girl? How do you know?"

"Duh! Because she disappeared and never returned, that's how. Where do you think she went? I had to get a lift home with Amy and Barb." Phoebe snapped her gum. "Just wait till I get my hands on that bitch."

"On Alynn?"

"No, doofus! On the bitch who swiped her!"

Craig fell back on his bed and smiled, eyes closed, returning to Doors rapture. Hah! So Alynn was as sly as she was beautiful. He couldn't wait for tomorrow evening. He'd never actually been with a girl before, but that didn't scare him a bit. He felt strong—stronger than he could remember. Like he could take on the world. He was intoxicated with it, drunk on the idea of this girl, this woman. He *was* Jim Morrison, and he sang louder. Didn't even notice his sister poking around his dresser, examining the folded place card.

★ ★ ★

"Now don't you look nice," said Amanda. She smiled sweetly as she admired her son from tip to toe. "Are you seeing that nice boy Jake again tonight?"

"No," said Craig, not bothering to correct her. He gave his mother a hug, glanced at his watch behind her apron. 9:25. He still had plenty of time. "I'm going to the arcade. Don't wait up."

"I thought you said you were studying tonight, big brother."

Craig caught the smoking gun of his sister's eyes from her perch on the couch.

"I'll study later," he said. And with that, he flipped his jacket over his shoulder, very cool, ran his hand through his hair and headed out the front door—Jim Morrison coming through. Almost knocked Johnna over as she entered unexpectedly.

"And just where are *you* going?" she asked.

"Arcade," he said, cool and suave, but smaller. He feared Johnna. She hadn't belted him in years, but his tower of apprehension stood erect.

"Don't stay out too late."

"But there's no school tomorrow, ma'am."

"Which is why I made a doctor's appointment for you."

"A doctor? But I'm not sick."

"Which is the way we want to keep it. Now run along, and be back at a decent hour."

"Yes, ma'am."

He walked to Amanda's car, got in and turned the ignition key, quickly dismissing any thoughts of Johnna's cold eyes or doctors, already gathering strength from his intended destination. He looked in the rear-view mirror and pushed back his hair with his hand.

The visitor's lot was poorly lit. He shut off the car, got out, locked the door, and looked at his watch. 9:45. Fifteen minutes early. He spotted another car in the lot. Good, he thought. She's early, too.

He walked the short distance to the bleachers. It was dark—much darker than the night before, a haze masking the star light and clouds blocking the stingy light cast by that shard of a moon. But as he neared the bleachers, he could see more clearly... There she was! But she wasn't alone. She was with someone, but who? No, there were *three* of them, and Alynn wasn't with them—

He stopped when he saw them, when they saw him, stopped cold, stopped dead as that familiar feeling rose up like a geyser, that adrenaline rush, a bubbling nausea. He stopped dead, terrified, just for an instant, then turned to run.

He knew they were chasing him—he could hear them. He was terrified. As he ran, his jaw chattered. When he reached his car, he slammed his shin against the bumper and the pain jabbed through his leg, but he ignored it. He was frantic for his keys—

But it was too late. They were on him.

They dragged him to the ground. Struggling was useless—they were terribly strong, pinning his arms behind him in a hammerlock. Craig tried to yell for help but someone grabbed his head and covered his mouth.

"Stop screaming you bastard!"

Craig recognized the voice, then doubled over as Jack's fist slammed him in the breadbasket, knocking the wind out of him.

"Please!" Craig cried. He thought he knew what was coming next, but he was wrong. Because he expected the beating—expected Jack, jilted Jack, enraged football jock Jack to get even for last night's sock in the eye.

He expected the kicking, the punching. But he was unprepared for what happened next.

By the time the third one finished, Craig wasn't even crying anymore.

★ ★ ★

A half hour passed. Craig sat there motionless, cold, numb, his face in his hands, sat alone in the cold night, his torn clothes caked with mud. He knew he was bleeding, but he didn't care. Didn't even bother to look up when he her voice.

"Are you alright?"

He didn't answer.

"I'm so sorry, Craig," said Alynn. "I couldn't help it. My neighbors went out and I was baby-sitting. I tried calling, but your mom said you'd already left."

Craig sat in silence, staring at the ground.

"Come on, Craig—don't be mad. I'm only twenty minutes late."

Slowly, he raised his head and looked up at her. That's when she noticed his bruised face. His eye had nearly swollen shut.

"Ohmygosh!" Alynn fell to her knees in front of Craig. "What happened?"

"I was raped," he said. And then he cried. And then they cried together.

After several minutes, Alynn helped Craig up, helped him to her car, then got in herself and began to drive.

"Where are we going?" he asked, his voice a faint rasp.

"Far away. I'm getting out of this horrible place once and for all. These people are *sick*! I can't stay here." She looked over at him. "Okay?"

He smiled. "Okay," he said. He began to feel a little better.

They drove for nearly an hour, his head on her shoulder, her right hand caressing his cheek, his hair. He watched the road signs change and become unfamiliar, then he saw a sign for the freeway. "Where are we going?" he asked.

"To Ontario. We can stay with my uncle. People there are more tolerant of people like us, people who are different."

"Different," he said. "I never thought of it that way. I always thought I was sick or something."

"Don't even say that, darling."

He smiled. Darling. "You know I'm in love with you," he said. "How can that be when we've only just met?"

Her soft hand caressed his face. "We were destined."

They drove for nearly five hours, each taking turns behind the wheel. It was Alynn's turn again. Craig sat beside her, his dream come true, that content feeling turning to giddiness as the night peeled back and the drunkenness of exhaustion pressed in.

It was almost 3:00 a.m. He yawned. "Let's pull over," he said. He placed his hand on her knee, no intention of going any further.

"Stop it," she said, pushing him away playfully.

He felt a rising tension in his loins, the push being an invitation of sorts. "Come on," he said. "Let's just cuddle for awhile." Gently, he returned his hand to her knee, higher this time. It was warm and soft.

"We're almost at the border," she said. "We can check into a hotel for the evening. Now stop touching me before I have an accident."

Craig grinned. It pleased him to know how he was affecting her. Thrilled him. He tickled the inside of her thigh with his thumb.

"C'mon—quit it," she said, giggling, squirming in the car seat, making the target irresistible. His fingers crept higher…

Suddenly, Craig shot back in his seat, gasping for breath.

"What a tease!" said Alynn. "Don't stop now. You're making my dick hard."

###

Clifford Meth was born Clifton Terrance O'Methany in County Clare, Ireland, on February 22, 1931, into an educated working class family. His father Mendel "Paddy" O'Methany, a.k.a. Paddy the Painter, a.k.a. Paddy Six Pockets, a.k.a. Big Paddy, a.k.a. Little Paddy, was a respected milkman and local poet who had been part of *Abisal Shicker*, the Jewish column of the Fenian Brotherhood during Ireland's War of Independence but was killed during the Troubles by a local prostitute over an etymological disagreement. Critics agree that memories of his father formed the basis of Meth's early work, in particular the seminal *In Search of My Drunken Tate* (Little Brown and Company, 1952) and the equally important sequel *Never Mind; He's Piss Drunk Again* (Rolling Stone Press, 1998).

Meth's political beliefs came from his mother, Mary Kathleen Sullivan, a personal friend of the Irish Republican Michael Collins. At the age of thirteen, in honor of his *bar-mitzvah*, Meth wrote a lament to Collins entitled *Du Momma Shtupper*, an allusion to the affectionate nickname his mother had given Collins.

Though Meth was a prominent activist, public speaker, actor, author, playwright, and seller of ladies' undergarments through most of his early career, his brother Brian did not share the same views, especially regarding the question of nationalism or how long to wait after *fleishiks*. This gives weight to the legend that Meth, at his brother's deathbed, asked Cathal Goulding (then Chief of Staff of the IRA), "Did you fart or is that Brian decomposing?"

Living alone in Wisconsin, Meth has not been active in the literary community for many years and *Billboards* is his first book in more than a decade. He has sworn vengeance on his enemies and apologizes if he hasn't gotten around to some of them yet.